FRAMED

Women in the Family Court Underworld

Dr. Christine Marie Cocchiola and Amy Polacko
Foreword by Dr. Ramani Durvasula

BETHLEHEM, CONNECTICUT

Framed: Women in the Family Court Underworld
© 2024, Dr. Christine Marie Cocchiola and Amy Polacko
All rights reserved.

Published by Narc Free Press, Bethlehem, Connecticut

ISBN 979-8-9907442-1-9 (paperback)
ISBN 979-8-9907442-0-2 (eBook)
Library of Congress Control Number: 2024913716

www.narcfreepress.com

This book is intended to provide accurate information with regard to its subject matter and reflects the opinion and perspective of the authors. However, in times of rapid change, ensuring all information provided is entirely accurate and up-to-date at all times is not always possible. Therefore, the authors and publisher accept no responsibility for inaccuracies or omissions and specifically disclaim any liability, loss, or risk, personal, professional, or otherwise, which may be incurred as a consequence, directly or indirectly, of the use and/or application of any of the contents of this book.

Publication managed by AuthorImprints.com

We dedicate this book to the brave women who contributed and to protective mothers and their children everywhere. Together, by sharing our stories, we will no longer be silenced.

CONTENTS

FOREWORD

By Ramani Durvasula, PhD

I remember the first time I heard someone call it the "divorce-industrial complex," a survivor of one of these divorces, who was an attorney, was talking with me about the many people who benefit financially from divorces. A multibillion-dollar enterprise that is almost incentivized to drag out marital dissolution and child custody decisions and fill the pockets of participants, including evaluators, consultants, experts, judges, and attorneys. Family court and the divorce and dissolution business are often easily gamed and weaponized by people driven by ego and entitlement, who believe the rules do not apply to them, who care more about winning, vindictiveness, power, and control than they care about the welfare not only of someone they once claimed to love, but of their children. Many a person has innocently walked into family court believing the decisions will be fair and balanced.

When a person is being harmed by someone who purportedly loves them, that person will blame themselves—relationships matter to healthy people, and attachment often means that survivors try to make sense of the abusive narrative within themselves and wonder what they are doing wrong. And this simple reversal is foundational for how people get stuck in harmful relationships for years, decades, even lifetimes. We are indoctrinated into the ideas that relationships are about compromise and sacrifice, that they are difficult, that they are work. Given that prevailing ideation, it is not surprising that people in these relationships not only assume that maybe "I am asking too much," exhaust themselves in trying to make them work but may also believe in the systems that are meant to support people going through these relationships and believe that these systems will "do the right thing."

When the abuse doesn't look like "abuse—when it is not broken bones and bruised faces—society is dismissive, despite growing research showing that the harms of emotional abuse are on par with all other forms of relational abuse, and emotional abuse is an inevitable piece of the picture of all abusive relationships. Even today, despite research on trauma and abuse, the reflexive response is to wonder what the "shared" responsibility is in a relationship, to ask people what they did to "provoke" the other person, that it takes "two to tango."

Dr. Cocchiola and I both agree that while all narcissistic or antagonistic people are not coercive controllers, all coercive controllers have these personalities. These are deceptive personalities—despite the invalidating, manipulative, fear-inducing behavior behind closed doors, these are people who can often either present in court as charming, smart, devoted parents, or as victims. Many people, who Dr. Cocchiola terms "protective parents" in coercively controlled relationships will go into court with what feels like clear evidence of the harms of this relationship, not only to have that evidence discounted, but also to be painted as a problematic or "alienating" parent. In addition, the courts rarely account for the significant emotional harm that happens to the protective parent, with the result that the safer parent often looks worn down or struggling with significant mental health challenges, thus propping up the narrative that the parent being harmed may be the "problem."

While the United Kingdom has been ahead of the United States regarding implementation of coercive control legislation, when this is tested in court it does not always work to protect children. For this reason, this book is crucially important— it matters more that you recognize these dynamics than necessarily trust the courts to identify these patterns. Without fail, every client I have ever clinically worked with as they traversed a divorce or separation from a narcissistic person has uttered the same words: "I feel insane." This book may help you develop better strategies with an attorney or advocate or shed more light on what you are experiencing to other people who care about you.

Coercive control represents a more severe behavioral pattern within narcissistic and antagonistic relationships. Some coercive dynamics show up in all narcissistic relationships—control, manipulation, gaslighting, jealousy—but in coercively controlled relationships these dynamics are more pervasive, consistent, menacing, and result in far more pronounced isolation and harm. However, when survivors understand that this is a "thing," it often strangely results in a sense of relief—a reminder that this is not a surreal, distorted universe that you are in alone—sadly, you are in good company.

We can read about the technical aspects of narcissism and coercive control repeatedly, but nothing has the impact of reading real people's stories. If you have experienced a coercively controlled relationship and feel as though you are in a dystopian universe, the stories and the insights in these pages will give you strategies, insights, validation, and a reminder that you are not alone. The authors do not sugarcoat this. While there have been some meaningful shifts in legislation, and occasionally, we do see some just outcomes, we continue to also observe how long-standing biases and consistent lack of integration of what we know about personality into decision-making by all of the players in the divorce-industrial complex. Whether you are living through this or you are a mental health practitioner or advocate who wants to learn more, this book will be a wake-up call, taking the concept of coercive control and giving it a face and a name.

TRIGGER WARNING

I f you've picked up this book, something intrigued you about it. Perhaps the title, or the cover. Or maybe you, or someone you love, a family member or a friend, has lived the experiences of the dark underworld of family court. If so, we are glad you are here. We hope this book validates that you are not alone—that no one is immune from this abuse. It can happen to anyone. It actually happens to many women.

We also hope you are someone who hasn't heard of this horrifying problem but is now interested and wants to learn more about it.

In either case, we want to warn you that the content in this book may be upsetting to some and also perhaps unbelievable. But we promise you that the stories you will read are the stories we and advocates all over the world hear every day. There truly is a dark underworld of the family court, of which most are blissfully unaware. We all know someone who has experienced this form of abuse—abuse from the confines of our home, far-reaching into years of vexatious litigation in the courthouse. We hope you will engage in self-care and call for support if you are overwhelmed by the content. Please call local emergency services or a domestic abuse hotline number if you or someone you know is unsafe.

GLOSSARY OF TERMS

Coercive control and domestic abuse: We prefer to use *domestic abuse* versus *domestic violence*. For far too long, our society has looked at abuse within a family system through the "violent incident model." This is archaic. Coercive control is the foundation of virtually all abuse—one person or group of people exerting power over another person or group of people, using both overt and covert tactics. Physical violence is not the defining characteristic. In coercive control, the exertion of power and control is the defining characteristic. Seeing domestic abuse, and all abuse, through the coercive control lens is foundational to our understanding the experiences of victims and survivors.

Coercive controller/narcissistic abuser: You will see us use these terms to describe abusers. As Dr. Ramani has affirmed in her foreword, not all narcissists are coercive controllers, but all coercive controllers are narcissistic abusers. These individuals are hell-bent on revenge and use whatever is within their reach to inflict significant harm on adult victims, and where there are children, they are victimized also.

Protective parent: For the purposes of this book, we will identify the parent who is the adult victim (target) of the coercive controller/narcissistic abuser as the "protective parent." The assumption is that this parent is healthy and has formed a secure attachment with their child.

Victims and survivors: We understand that some individuals do not like to identify as a victim or even as a survivor. However, our intent is to shed light on the experiences of these protective parents and their children as victims of coercive controllers/narcissistic abusers. Our attempt to elevate the victimization is intentional to remove the shame that all too often is placed on the victim. Pivoting to the perpetrator is our goal.

Solicitors and barristers: In the United Kingdom and in Australia, there may be two individuals who fulfill the role of an attorney. Solicitors complete the preparation work before court appearances, including providing legal advice, drafting contracts, and negotiating settlements. They will also determine if a case is contentious or non-contentious. Barristers are often hired by solicitors to represent a case in court. Barristers specialize in making court appearances and speaking on behalf of the client, handling the more specific and complex aspects of the case.

This book is a compilation of stories about mothers as victims, since domestic abuse in all its forms is primarily a male-identifying perpetration against female-identifying victims. Coercive control takes shape around the prevalence of male dominance and their superior positions relative to women, with tactics often reflective of historical gender norms; therefore, women are at far greater risk of victimization when compared to men (Stark 2007). We acknowledge that there are instances of female-identifying perpetration against male-identifying victims; however, these circumstances are less frequent and often less egregious. The systems complicit in these harms are formed in patriarchal norms, and in that, as research affirms, there is a greater oppression of mothers versus fathers.

PREFACE

lose your eyes and imagine if you can for a minute that you're in the safety of your home, perhaps enjoying dinner and laughter with your children, when there's a thunderous knock on the door.

It's the police.

They say you are wanted for questioning in an investigation. What? You haven't been in trouble with the law since you got a speeding ticket at age seventeen—and that was over thirty years ago. You are a model citizen with a responsible job and track record as a stable, loving mother. But on this night, you must come with the police and leave your kids in the care of another, leaving them wondering if their mother will ever return.

Your only "crime"? You want a divorce.

This isn't a nocturnal nightmare you eventually wake up from. Or one extreme story that's an anomaly in our justice system. This is happening in America—and beyond—every single day. You have lived with this fear every day for months or perhaps years now.

Always wondering when and if your ex will implement the revenge he is always threatening.

Our cultural norms tell us to "call for help" and "just leave" if we're experiencing abuse at home. We grow up with this underlying message from our institutions—such as the police, our courts, and social service organizations—that "we'll protect you" once you make that jump to freedom. Isn't this what we tell our kids? And isn't having this safety net why we pay our taxes?

But the police tell you you're accused of abusing your spouse, endangering your children, or harassing your ex-partner's new romantic interest. The room starts spinning and you try to defend yourself, but it becomes painfully clear the investigators don't believe you. And when you're in family court, the same *Twilight Zone* moment happens over and over again. You report the abuse you've suffered at the hands of your spouse, but no one seems to care. In fact, you are accused of fabricating the story and alienating your children from the abuser.

You, my friend, are the villain of this story. And your abuser's portrayal of you as "crazy" will prove almost impossible to shake. Who buys into this scheme? Your spouse's attorney, parental evaluators, attorneys for the children in custody disputes, advocates who fall prey to the false narratives of abusers claiming victim—and yes, even judges.

You are framed.

You might think this kind of thing only happens in countries with inferior judicial systems. Family courts always give custody of the children to the mother—unless she's a drug addict or mentally ill—so the societal myth says. Everyone in our country has the right to counsel, even if they can't afford one, right? Wrong. Wrong. And wrong.

For instance, the Sixth Amendment in the US Constitution only provides *criminal* defendants with the right to a free lawyer. If you're a litigant in family court, up against a spouse with millions to spend waging a war against you, you're on your own. And most protective parents will sell their belongings, house, and even the clothes off their backs to defend themselves and try to protect their children. Some we know end up homeless, jobless, and destitute. They're fighting a losing battle, as George Washington University Law Professor Joan Meier and team revealed in her seminal 2019 study "Custody Outcomes in Cases Involving Parental Alienation and Abuse Allegations." Of the 1,137 cases where mothers alleged domestic violence, courts sided with women in only 517 cases—that's 45 percent. Of the 200 cases where mothers accused fathers of child sexual abuse, courts believed moms only 15 percent of the time.

We, as a clinical therapist and divorce coach, work with these women every single day. Their partners are bent on revenge, control, and power at any cost. They are coercive controllers/narcissistic abusers—and their campaign can take the form of psychological abuse such as gaslighting, manipulation, intimidation, and isolation, financial abuse, legal abuse, and of course their favorite tactic, the weaponization of the children. They use family court as the ultimate tool to do so. In some cases, they file motions against their spouse almost daily with the court docket reaching in the hundreds. It's called "The Abuser's Playbook" and it is designed to destroy their ex-partner legally, financially, and psychologically.

The scariest part? Our family court system doesn't just let them get away with it but hands them the tricks and tools to wage their war. As Bandy Lee, psychiatrist and advocate for child safety, tells us, "criminal courts must abide by the law and strict rules of procedure, family courts are not only a secret but a lawless land, where the judge can put anyone in jail without due process, bail, or even cause" (Lee 2024). This lawless land is where mothers go to jail for attempting to protect their children. It is a dystopian world.

In our work, we support victims and survivors. In short, we believe them and give them the space to share their stories without any judgment. Escaping these situations is no easy feat, and oftentimes the psychological mind games make leaving seem impossible. Dr. Evan Stark likened coercive control to carpenter ants devouring the foundation of a house. You don't even know it is happening until it is too late. Yet our society asks all the time, "Why did she stay?" Our work is focused on ensuring victims and survivors know they are not alone and that there are strategies they can learn to support both them and their children. That's whether they are choosing to stay (because it feels safer), trying to plan for the escape, or after they have finally broken free. It is entrapment.

What makes us uniquely qualified to do this work isn't just our degrees, certifications, and professional experience. It's this: We have lived in these women's shoes. We answered the door when the police came knocking. We faced the misogynist tropes in our justice system that painted us as the "unhinged" ones. We are still reeling from the deep, cutting betrayal by the institutions that were supposed to protect us. We tried to shield our children from the chaos our ex-spouses created. We faced divorce in a broken legal system that favors the abuser. And we are still healing every single day.

This is why we are writing this book.

As so many say, when you experience what happens in family court firsthand, you simply cannot look away. You must go back and lift up the next woman who's trying desperately to survive.

If you are blissfully unaware of how simply wanting a divorce can put you into the battle of your lifetime—which will try you mentally, emotionally, and financially like you never have been before—we are happy for you. We hope you never face this hell. But someone you know has been or is living this nightmare. We can promise you that. So, we need your help. Read these stories, share them, and work with us to shine a light on this human rights crisis that even had the United Nations Human Rights Council's Special Rapporteur speak out in June 2023 against family courts' dangerous gender bias. The world is noticing.

And if you have lived, or are living, in this trauma we describe, please know you have a special place in our hearts. Your stories drive us. They help us get out of bed in the morning and continue this work day after day. A special thank-you to the women who so generously shared their stories for this book. Regardless of the fact that most are told anonymously and many details are changed, it took a tremendous amount of courage.

Let their bravery inspire us—to work together to increase awareness, to pressure our legislators into passing laws that curtail abusers' ability to continue abusing in family court, to hold our judges and all family court professionals accountable, to protect innocent children, and to support the true victims of domestic abuse.

Call us dreamers, but we're working toward a world where no woman will ever be framed again. After you read these stories, we hope you will join us too.

INTRODUCTIONS

By Christine Marie Cocchiola, DSW, LCSW

As a concept, outside of academia and in the general public, coercive control has only recently begun to gain traction among professionals who work with individuals who have experienced domestic abuse. Perhaps some of you reading this book have not heard of the concept of coercive control.

Cases such as that of Evan Rachel Wood, actor and ex-girlfriend of Marilyn Manson, Amber Heard and Johnny Depp, and Gabby Petito, who was murdered during a cross-country trip with her boyfriend, have shone a light on this lesser-understood underpinning of abuse, as has the #MeToo movement and related activism.

Coercive control, now widely known to be the foundation of all domestic abuse, includes tactics that encompass the realm of psychological torture and the diminishing of an individual's autonomy.

I see coercive control as the underpinning of *all* abuse with one individual or a group of individuals exerting power over another or others, using a victim's vulnerabilities against them. It occurs in intimate relationships, but as you will see from these stories, oftentimes the systems are complicit.

Physical violence is not the defining characteristic of coercive control. A pattern of coercion and control is the defining characteristic of coercive control. This exertion of power crosses time and space, happening both within and outside of the relationship. It is often nuanced and insidious with the intent to diminish a victim's autonomy. It may be overt or covert and abusers do not discriminate. It's not an exaggeration to liken it to terrorism, and experts who have investigated the mind-bending reality of prisoners of war call it exactly that.

Perpetrators—coercive controllers/narcissistic abusers—will often use other forms of abuse, including financial, legal, and sexual abuse, along with the weaponization of children, often the most heartbreaking tactic of abuse. Abusive partners and parents often present as stable and well intentioned, when in fact they are not. Children living in these situations are suffering unacknowledged child abuse. The perpetrator is the only individual at fault.

Enter the family court. In family court, abuse victims suffer invisibility every day with a judicial system that fails to acknowledge this pattern of coercion and control. The dark underbelly of the family court often goes unnoticed behind the veneer of what we assume are educated individuals making decisions based on the best interests of children. Yet this is often not the case. There is a disconnect and a level of arrogance—

or simply put, complicitness—with court professionals failing to acknowledge that domestic abuse and child abuse are not siloed issues.

Abusive parents often participate in neglectful or overindulgent parenting. Or worse, their omnipotence is evident to everyone in the family system. The fear is palpable to the discerning eye. Abusers also very often indoctrinate children into a false narrative against the protective parent. Here, in family court, an abuser can use virtually every tactic of coercive control with the support of court professionals, who are oftentimes either none the wiser about the abuser's intentions and disordered character traits or simply arrogant and sit by idle, ignoring the plight of adult and child victims. Many of us in the field wonder about the level of complicit "actors." It's hard to imagine it could be true, but there seems to be no other explanation.

The belief that "it takes two to tango" or the situation is "high-conflict" permeates, yet there is only one person who is drawn toward conflict, the abuser (Rosenfeld et al. 2019). Using the judicial system to exert this control becomes the ultimate weapon, with the coercive control often intensifying in what is now widely known as post-separation abuse (Sharps-Jeffs, Kelly, and Klein 2017). The abuser's mantra: If I cannot control you, I will control the systems intended to protect you to control you. This is institutional betrayal, with complex and compound trauma being the end result.

The latter is what myself and co-author and dear friend Amy Polacko, along with other advocates, see all too often. A family court system that actually gives abusers the "stage" to further exert their coercion and control with everyone in the family system, including the children, who are the ultimate weapon.

You may ask, why doesn't a protective parent and her attorney tell the court what is occurring? Often attorneys and court professionals are not invested in victims' experiences. The family court process is profitable. And there is a "good ole boys" club that permeates due to patriarchy. When abuse is covert, it is challenging for victims themselves to recognize their own loss of autonomy. And even when there is overt coercive control, in the form of physical violence or sexual violence, verbal assaults, and stalking, the experiences are diminished by family court, with adult victims of abuse disbelieved for their own abuse and disbelieved at a greater rate when the perpetrator has abused the children.

When adult victims—protective parents—bring forth allegations of abuse, coercive controllers/narcissistic abusers will often co-opt the term *parental alienation* to gain the sympathy of judges and lawyers performing for the court. Kate Manne (2018) coined the term *himpathy*, which describes the disproportionate sympathy extended to a male perpetrator in cases of sexual assault, harassment, and other misogynistic behavior. Taking the term a step further, himpathy applies well to what we see in family court. A father who expresses an interest in protective parenting receives an inordinate amount of himpathy. Yet a mother's desire to protect her children is seen in an unequal light. If the father alleges that he is being "alienated," regardless of whether there is evidence of his being a protective parent, he is often able to take custodial time away from a protective mother and, in the worst cases, remove custody from a protective mother. Parental alienation becomes weaponized in order to exert the greatest harm via the judicial system, forcing children into the care of an abusive parent.

The argument used for ignoring coercive control within the family system is the notion that all parents have a right to their children and that all parents have their children's best interests in mind. This simply is not true. Coercive controllers/narcissistic abusers only have an intent to retain control of the adult victim. The children are weaponized to do this—with the court as ammunition.

This is not an anomaly. As a social justice advocate since the age of nineteen, volunteering for a local domestic abuse/sexual assault agency, a child welfare worker, and a clinician, I have heard these stories daily throughout my career. Dr. Evan Stark described the children living in these situations as secondary victims, not because their abuse is less significant, but because they, the children, are irrelevant to the abusive parent. The only role of the children is that of a choice weapon to harm the protective parent (Stark 2023).

Research affirms that children in these families are beyond witnesses of the abuse, suffering at the hands of the perpetrators, whether the abuse is overt or covert. Intimate terrorism is difficult to explain or discern, like a cult, with family members lining up to adhere to the abuser's criteria simply to survive.

It is hard to imagine that an individual would behave with such malicious intent to someone they supposedly love. Most of us take responsibility for (wrong) actions and then shift behaviors in an attempt to make amends and to improve our relationships. Coercive controllers/narcissistic abusers count on this. They count on victims being agreeable and conscientious, and this is how they continue to further entrap their victims, making them smaller and smaller, with the victim's agency lost. It is death by a thousand cuts.

These perpetrators often project what they do onto others; their accusation is often their confession. Shame becomes impossible to handle, and coercive controllers/narcissistic abusers must do everything to diminish this shame, even if it means harming those they profess to love by projecting that shame onto others. The others are anyone who does not align with the abuser, and anyone the abuser can shed his shame onto.

To be perfectly clear, it is a nightmare resulting in the most horrifying of circumstances, particularly because we know that physical violence, when it occurs, is not the worst part. Victims will spend years questioning their reality, gaslit into believing they are the problem. This understanding is affirmed with Albert Biderman's research during the Korean War and his creation of the Chart of Coercion, which describes the stress manipulation tactics used to elicit false confessions (1957). Under a totalitarian communist regime, prisoners of war could be worn down and eventually acquiesce and even align with their oppressors. As psychologists tell us, the human condition can be easily manipulated with so much at stake.

The reality is that whether the abuse is overt or covert, it is often nuanced and insidious. Even the most astute of us may miss the signs. I certainly did.

I was drawn to social work at a young age because someone I love had been abused as a child. I naively had the lofty goal of eradicating the abuse of our most vulnerable. I loved that the philosophy of social work is based upon looking at the human condition through the lens of the human environment. What occurs in the home that is harmful to the developing child can very much impact the trajectory of life for that child. This was in the early '90s, well before Gabor Maté's work was mainstream, Bessel van der Kolk's *The Body Keeps Score*, Vincent Filetti's Adverse Childhood Experiences (ACEs) Study, Judith Herman's seminal book, *Trauma and Recovery*, plus Bruce Perry and Oprah Winfrey's *What Happened to You?* Their work, along with the work of many other researchers, affirm that behavior is the language of trauma. *Children will show us how they feel before they tell us how they feel.*

I became obsessed with understanding trauma and the harm inflicted on children in family systems where abuse was occurring. I saw this in my daily work as a child welfare social worker. I knew clearly the impact on children in these family systems, with domestic abuse the common thread in so many child welfare cases. I devoured as much information as possible on the subject and created various trainings for educators and advocates on the signs of trauma in children and best practices to support children manifesting this trauma in their behaviors. I began teaching social work courses through the trauma lens, again before many were talking about the impact of ACEs and the trauma that many have experienced in their childhood.

All the while, I didn't know this was happening in my own relationship. I knew I was unhappy in my home life. I loved being a mother, but I was all too often anxious. I went to therapy in an attempt to fix me. I was always wondering, *What could I do differently? How can I be a better person, wife, and mother?* Again, as mentioned in the preface, the carpenter ants were devouring away the foundation of my home, and I didn't know it was happening. Before I would figure it out, it would be too late.

Abusers often show up as charlatans—a wolf in sheep's clothing. Like in a cult, their victims fall in line. In intimate relationships, there are often the initial experiences of intense love and acceptance. Our brain has a neurological response—oxytocin, the cuddle hormone, and other hormones—fortifying a trauma bond. Research affirms that trauma bonding consists of strong, relation-based emotional ties between an abuser and victim, which are reinforced through positive and negative experiences (Dutton and Painter 1981; 1993). Trauma bonds are not easily broken. Frequently described as akin to a substance use addiction, the abusive behaviors with intermittent positive experiences reinforce the attachments, with victims seeking experiences that are positive and requiring less of these positive experiences as time goes on. As Simonic and Osweska (2019) explain victims often have distorted beliefs and behavioral strategies that prevent "seeing" the truth, or recognizing it (86). These distortions are never a victim's fault—they are created as a result of the coercion and control inflicted by the perpetrator—a stripping away of a victim's autonomy. This loss of agency diminishes their ability to see the abuse for what it is, often persisting in hopes that the relationship will improve. Victims become blind to the betrayal.

I persisted. Victims and survivors tend to be fixers—optimistic, loyal, and forgiving— and willing to see the best in others even when coercive controllers/narcissistic abusers continue to show them their worst. I kept working on myself. Of course this is exactly what abusers hope for. I was perfect prey, as are so many of the protective parents I coach and support.

Thankfully, I had a very fulfilling career, the love and support of extended family, and a core group of friends that I could lean on. My mom and dad and siblings were there without judgment each and every time I considered escaping the relationship. I would draw on these three positive parts of my life during my darkest hours. More than that, I had my children. For their sake, I realized that, in my case, escaping the abuse might be the best way for them to gain clarity. You see, like so many protective parents, I didn't want my children to suffer, and I certainly didn't want them to think that something was wrong with their family. In my attempt to protect them, I protected the abuser. They were living in the same fog that I lived in for years, except, as with all children of coercive control, their experiences were even more compromising due to their stages of development. The fog lifted when the abuser turned on them.

According to a report by the World Health Organization (WHO), nearly 1 in 3 women (about 33%) have been subjected to physical or sexual violence by an intimate partner (2024). These are the violent cases. What of the cases that are not considered violent? If three women a day were mauled by a bear, we would be calling it a crisis, yet violence against women is not discussed or recognized as the epidemic that it is. Domestic abuse is the number one killer of African American women ages fifteen to thirty-five (Rice et al. 2022). Girls and young women ages sixteen to twenty-four are at the greatest risk, suffering abuse three times greater than the United States national average (Bureau of Justice Statistics 2001).

This is not about us (women) versus them (men) or a we-versus-them problem. This is an issue that impacts all of us, men and women, boys and girls, gays, lesbians, bisexuals, nonbinary individuals, Black, white, or brown. The oppression of one person or group of people based on another person or group of people having power over them is harmful to each living being. Dr. Stark called coercive control a liberty crime. bell hooks defined feminism as the "struggle to eliminate all forms of oppression" (1984). Gender oppression ends, an oppression that impacts all of humanity and most significantly, impacts our most vulnerable, when all oppression ends.

Coercive control is structurally endemic. It does not only occur in intimate relationships. It crosses all spheres. Coercive control is embedded in our policies and in the systems that implement these policies. It thrives in the very systems that we all rely on for protection.

Due to the social and political constructs of our society, inclusive of patriarchal norms, women and children are the most defenseless against and susceptible to a perpetrator's exertion of power and control over them. Coercive control is a crime against humanity.

As a therapist and a parenting coach, I want to spread the word: It is a myth that children need a two-parent home. What children do need is to feel safe from all harms, overt or covert, and to receive unconditional love with the ability to be authentically accepted as they are. These relationship dynamics create a secure attachment and are vital to a child's well-being. Perpetrators will do anything to maliciously fracture this attachment. My passion is to support protective parents and allies with clinical interventions and parenting strategies necessary to fortify this attachment—even when the abuser is working double time to fracture it.

Too often court professionals and even therapists miss or entirely ignore the signs of coercive control within the parental subsystem and railroad a child's attachment to their protective parent. This must change. I was lucky that I didn't endure a custody battle. Had I left sooner, I'm certain it would have occurred. I did suffer mockery and abuse by court professionals; even my own lawyer made fun of me. I was gaslit by therapists and advocates who pressed me to do more for the relationship and more for the abuser, when I had already sacrificed my whole self to him. Victims are often asked to do this—to sacrifice themselves and their children—all for a perpetrator whose only intent is to harm.

We need to recognize coercive control within intimate relationships and, beyond that, within our systems. We need to acknowledge coercive control as the child abuse it is. We must prevent the trauma so our children do not carry it to the next generation.

As Maya Angelou told us, "There is no greater agony than bearing an untold story inside of you." These are the stories of the bravest women that you will ever come to know. In reading these stories, perhaps you can, to some degree, imagine yourself as these women, as these mothers. And then imagine the ravages by the systems—the very systems we all rely upon for protection. What if this was you? Or your mother, sister, daughter, friend, or worse, your child living in this horror? Would it be your call to action?

We hope that seeing yourself as these mothers will bring you to work collectively with us to end this oppression. Once you see it, you cannot unsee it.

By Amy Polacko

The text made me freeze in my tracks—and my son never misses a thing.

"What's the matter, Mom?" he asked.

I smiled and shook my head so he wouldn't worry as we walked down a Connecticut beach with friends on the Saturday of Memorial Day weekend in 2023.

"Amy," the message read, "the woman you wrote about is saying she is committing suicide."

"Check your email," said another.

I felt sick, sat down, and started frantically scrolling back to the morning. It was unusual that I had not read my emails, but it was a holiday weekend and we had been driving to the beach.

Catherine.

I had been planning a follow-up story on her case and felt like an elephant had landed on my chest. I found the email entitled "My Story" from Catherine Kassenoff that began with the sentence that still haunts her supporters to this day: "This is a story that ends with my own assisted death in Switzerland."

I had written the first story on Catherine's family court case for *Ms.* magazine in December of 2021 entitled, "Empty Home for the Holidays: Mothers Who Can't See Their Children Blame Broken Family Court System." In it, I profiled Catherine of Westchester County, New York, and Cobie Jane of Fairfield County, Connecticut—two mothers who had lost custody of their children after reports of alleged abuse by their husbands.

I, like so many others, desperately responded to Catherine—told her I was so sorry she had come to this, implored her to rethink the decision, and reminded her what a bright light she was for so many. Sadly, our entreaties did not work.

"My husband made an ex parte motion to evict me from my home and a judge signed it," this bright attorney, who was then a special counsel for New York Governor Kathy Hochul, told me back then. "He argued that I have a mental illness, I'm a liar, and I put my children up to make false reports about him. I was evicted immediately—even though a detective testified that my daughters were extremely credible." After years in court not seeing her three daughters, it looked like Catherine was getting some wins (including having a forensic evaluator removed from the case) and finally had unsupervised visits with her girls. But in 2023, Catherine said a new forensic evaluator rubber stamped an old report and she was suspended from any visits yet again. That was the final blow.

In her goodbye email, Catherine wrote:

> *The New York Court system is responsible for this outcome and should be held accountable for ruining the lives of my children, me, and so many other similarly-situated protective parents (mostly mothers) who have tried to stand up against abuse but were labeled 'liars,' 'mentally ill' and then treated like criminals. The reason the courts engaged in this horror, where they 'temporarily' took away custody, my personal property, a home I owned and lived in, my*

dogs, my health, my career, and my dignity—for the last 4 years—was so that the nearly $4 million that Allan Kassenoff, my ex-husband, had to spend to destroy me could be handed out to the court appointed forensics, therapists, lawyers for the children and the attorney for Kassenoff. It is a disgrace that persists under the cloak of secrecy and 'off the record' court proceedings, secret forensic reports, and 'ex parte' applications and orders.

I wrote several follow-up articles for *Ms.* about Catherine's death and family court injustice—including one on what would happen to her children, another on how this human rights crisis should alarm America and the world, and an accusation by legal experts that "emergency" family court orders violate the due process guaranteed in the Constitution. Her husband did not respond to our requests for an interview in 2023. The first story after her death was the most-read story in *Ms.* magazine in 2023. Thousands of women—and a few men—contacted me with their horrific custody stories from across the country and around the globe. Catherine's story spread on social media like wildfire, inspiring the hashtags #CatherineKassenoff and #IamCatherine. Many of us hoped that we were reaching a watershed moment like #MeToo. We were wrong.

That's why I'm writing this book with my colleague and friend Dr. Christine Cocchiola. That's why I continue to shine a light on this underworld in my small way as a journalist. I am also a divorce coach who helps women navigate what can be a nightmare, and

95 percent of my clients are victims of coercive control. Everyone who's survived an abusive relationship has their own path to healing. As a former full-time investigative reporter on television, using my journalistic skills to raise awareness about narcissistic abusers and family court has been a key part of mine.

I have been divorced twice so I'm no stranger to this justice system—and, as I always say: Once you've been to family court, trust me, you will never be the same.

I was a babe in the woods when I went up against a high-conflict partner in family court. Just like so many women, we grow up thinking our justice system is there to protect us. Many of us go through life with no contact with this system—until we go through a divorce. It's only then that we experience the double standards, misogyny, and "richest take all" forces that dominate this underworld. Our brains struggle to process the depth of this duplicity.

When the masks begin to come off our narcissistic partners, we often experience cognitive dissonance, which is the perception of contradictory information and the mental toll of that. For me, I started to put the pieces together after googling *pathological liar* and came up with articles on narcissists and sociopaths. My ex-partner lied about everything—where he was, money, relationships with other women—but gaslighted me every time I confronted him. If I dared to express how I felt, I got the silent treatment—or worse. As a victim, you start to question your own intuition and find yourself walking on eggshells every single day. Just when you're about to walk away, abusers sense this and love bomb you all over again to keep you tethered to them. To maintain control. That's why it takes abuse victims' brains, like mine, time to fully accept that the very person we fell in love with is actually out to destroy us.

Likewise, when our family court system is not only indifferent to our abuse—and that of our children—and enables the coercive controller/narcissistic abuser to weaponize it against us, we experience cognitive dissonance again. This hits victims with a secondary trauma that can be even more devastating: institutional betrayal. That's when an institution causes harm to the very people who depend on it.

The concept was developed by Dr. Jennifer Freyd, founder and president of the Center for Institutional Courage, who has studied this subject for decades. "Institutional betrayal can occur through ignorance, meaning you don't have to wake up with evil thoughts to cause harm. You can cause harm because you're ignorant and don't understand interpersonal violence," she said in an October 23, 2023 *Ms.* magazine piece I wrote on "'Hysterical' Women Out for Revenge: Family Court's Misogynistic Tropes Traumatize Women and Children." "Betrayal is really damaging. It adds so much risk to people—causing them to get post-trauma symptoms to their physical health and mental health. It's toxic."

This deep trauma can even cause people to attempt suicide, Freyd said. Catherine Kassenoff stated clearly that the family court system's betrayal is what drove her to assisted suicide. And her own attorney admitted that the court labeled her as "unhinged" for being persistent in pursuit of her girls. I have to ask: Who wouldn't be a bit disturbed if their children were taken from them?

The thousands of women I've talked to—interview subjects for stories, coaching clients, members of my support group, and those who have emailed me their stories—all say the same thing: There was a bias against them and their credibility from the very beginning.

When a retired court official bragged in front of me about how much money she was making mediating divorce cases, I thought I was in the *Twilight Zone*. When I was asked, "Why do you have to call yourself a victim?" it baffled and angered me—this by someone who had read my attorney's painstaking history of the domestic abuse/coercive control I had suffered. I, like so many other women, was told to just "go with the flow." Your ex didn't submit his financials as required? Don't rock the boat! You think all the psychological and financial abuse you've suffered should be considered? Nobody cares.

Now that I'm a divorce and post-separation abuse coach, I'm on a mission to educate others about this system—and warn them. I even created a comprehensive digital course called "Divorce Decoded" that includes family court warnings women are not getting anywhere else and must know as they enter this arena. My July 2023 essay in *HuffPost* called "I Help People Get Divorced. I'm Begging You—Don't Ignore These Red Flags Before Marrying" set out to caution the naive, using stories from my clients who are stuck in hell. One woman was jailed under false charges; another was at the beach with her kids when a court officer called to say her ex was trying to have her committed so she had to appear on video immediately to defend herself. The response I got from this article was overwhelming, with many people saying "you were telling my family court story too" and "I had no idea there were more of us out there."

Sandy Ross, a child safety advocate, said she hoped we are seeing an inflection point, when she spoke to me for my "'Hysterical' Women Out for Revenge" article. "I strongly believe the tide is turning," Ross said. "Finally, we are getting worldwide attention—even from the UN—and the issue is rising to a level where it cannot be ignored."

Let's hope Sandy is right. In the meantime, we owe it to people who have no idea what they're about to encounter in family court to educate them. We owe it to people embroiled in a legal battle with an abuser to support them. And we owe it to the general public to expose them to injustices many legal experts say use millions of taxpayer dollars. It is a violation of American civil rights and due process plus human rights everywhere (see my *Ms.* article "Lawyers Say Catherine Kassenoff's Case—and Thousands of Others—Violate U.S. Constitutional Right to Due Process").

Catherine Kassenoff is far from the only parent who's lost custody of their children and then taken their own life. She's just the only one I knew personally.

My and my dear friend and colleague Dr. Cocchiola's hope is that maybe, just maybe, by writing this book—and including the stories of real women—we can help prevent another protective parent from reaching the breaking point. Our message to you is this: You are not alone. We are out here fighting for you every single day.

And if you're not a protective parent, what can you do? Please help us educate others, support those being "framed," and fight for change by sharing this book. Post a link to it on social media or buy a copy and send it to a friend who could benefit from our message. Women must be encouraged to keep telling their stories.

Because every time a survivor tells her story, it helps heal someone else.

FAIRY TALE GONE WRONG

Cathy's Story – United States

W e met in the early nineties. I was a year out of college and he was a couple of years older. There was an immediate spark even though I was not looking to date anybody. We really seemed to connect, continued to date, and we seemed... to fall hard for each other. After a few months, Ian introduced me to his family and invited me to a sibling's wedding. Apparently, it was the first time he'd ever introduced a girlfriend to the family.

It was a bit of a whirlwind and seemed to be going well—sort of. We were head over heels, but there were certain things that would pop up that I would question. Comments he would make. One of my good friends said Ian was very arrogant, and I always felt that he was trying to control the time we spent together. But what did I know? It was my first long-term relationship out of school.

He would say we can go out one night per weekend, and the other night, he was with his friends. Then, maybe seven or eight months in, he said that he loved me but he was not ready to get married. Who the hell wanted to get married? I was just about to embark on a career and more. But he broke up with me. There was always this weird connection and longing—for both of us— he'd say. Every once in a while, I would bump into him out at night and we would be like magnets drawn to each other. He drew me in. It was a euphoria that I had felt the first night we met, and I thought this must be *that* connection that people talk about. The one.

Even though I was not ready to get married at all, we just kept connecting. After a few months, we got back together because as he said, "I just can't stay away from you." In hindsight, there were so many things that he had said and done that were subtle put-downs and twisted comments. For instance, one time he stopped over and left a note because I wasn't home. The note read, "Looks like you missed me!" A normal person would usually say, "Sorry I missed you."

There were always twisted words and situations. One day, when we were either breaking up or getting back together, I remember him saying to me that one of his concerns was he didn't know if I would be a good mother. I remember thinking, *What the hell?* Many people have told me I'm one of the most caring, maternal people they know. I come from a long line of incredibly strong, nurturing women. I think this is one of the most outrageous things someone has said to me to date. And this was a person who supposedly was madly in love with me! But somehow it was so shocking, I thought maybe there was something wrong. How could this person even consider not being with me because they think I would not be a good mother? Of course, I would prove him wrong. It's painful just thinking about it now, honestly.

I ended up becoming roommates with one of his friend's girlfriends the second year we were dating and had gotten back together. His friend was absolutely borderline psychotic, basically stalking my friend, listening to our answering machine messages, waiting outside the door, etc. Scary. But I think back to the eighties, nineties, and even a few years ago, and we all thought that abuse meant you had a black eye or a broken arm from someone. We would say they're just psycho or an asshole. So, it was a little crazy, but we kept moving forward.

Looking back, I remember there were just so many people surrounding his situation that seemed a bit unhealthy and off. But there were also nights going out having fun and, of course, I was head over heels in love. On nights that we didn't hang out together, I was always waiting to hear what was happening, where he was, when we would get together, and more. He was always keeping me guessing just a little, and the undertone was that I was clingy, trying to be controlling, and that I was the luckiest person in the world.

Another few months went by and he broke up again. I was heartbroken, and this happened one other time spanning another year. Breaking up yet "so in love" that we were pulled back together. It was crazy-making to me. I felt devastated, like a part of me was ripped out. The good times were so emotionally bonding, like he had reached deep into my being and connected.

And he would say so. Now when I look back, it was deliberate manipulation and mind games.

The last breakup came the day before Valentine's Day after we had spent the whole night together. He just said he wasn't ready for all this. Again. I was so devastated. I ended up dating someone else for almost a year, but always longing for him, always comparing how much more fun it would be if we were together, no matter what I was doing. Again, we bumped into each other once in a while—magnets. He would say things like he couldn't stop thinking about me, I was the most amazing person, the most beautiful person in the room, and we're supposed to be together.

I ended up moving to New York City and, out of the blue, on Valentine's Day, he showed up with a dozen roses at my apartment—sucking me right back in with all the romance of a fairytale. The one all the little girls dream of—including me. I was pulled back in again! The subtle lies, doubts, and manipulation, sugar-coated with acts of grand gestures, left me completely confused and living on a roller-coaster ride of complete and utter fairy-tale love, plus days and nights of sadness and confusion. There were many middle-of-the-night, angry phone calls because I had waited for hours when he was supposed to come and meet me or call me. There was always an excuse. It seems crazy now when I think back to what I accepted and what seemed to make sense.

I was also now in the middle of an amazing, exciting career. He was never jealous, it seemed— always encouraging me to work late hours. My career came with a lot of advantages like high-profile events and more. Interestingly, many years later when we were breaking up, friends and family started coming to me with little stories or insights that they had. One of them was that he would always brag and boast about not me but how cool it was, all the people he met and the things he did. They were all because of me . . . but it wasn't framed that way and I wasn't mentioned.

The push and pull was like a yo-yo. I remember thinking way deep down in my gut this isn't working, that it didn't feel right. We never moved in together. I really felt that I shouldn't lose my freedom until I was really making a commitment to someone for life. I had great roommates and I still liked my time alone, whether it was by my choice or not.

He mentioned we should go to Europe on vacation. Of course, that sounded wonderful to me. So, we did. And we got engaged there. I really wasn't expecting it, especially the romance of it all. He had spoken to my family about it and had received their blessing. At that moment, it was like a dream. And when we called family to share the news, God as my witness, I had a pit in my stomach. I felt it on and off for the rest of the trip. But I shoved that feeling way, way down.

I never admitted this to myself, or anybody, until maybe eight years ago. Through all three breakups that he prompted, I repressed all my feelings and knowledge that this wasn't right. But, with all the grand gestures and love bombing—a big, amazing wedding with our families and friends, followed by three kids—it was a whirlwind.

I worked through the first two kids dealing with basically everything. Again, hindsight sparked aha moments of such outrageous manipulation and abuse of my feelings. Silent treatment for days. We went to therapists, he had conversations with family and friends about how much he wanted us to work, and we worked on it. He would say I was just exhausted, angry, overly sensitive, disorganized, and not flexible about any decisions. It's so sickening when I think of all the things that I ignored and how twisted my brain, my heart, and my entire being was from his psychological abuse.

It wasn't as apparent or insidious in my day-to-day world because I was busy around the clock. I had my kids all the time. Even with my job, I never missed an appointment or a school event and I ran back and forth every single day. I was so busy, I didn't really have time to analyze him. I just thought he was being a jerk and had some issues. All the therapists talked in circles, and he would hold on to one thing they said that might validate his feelings a bit, and I wouldn't hear the end of it for weeks and weeks. He would also broadcast that thing to friends and family.

We had dated on and off for over six years and were married for almost ten when there was parental illness, and we had to move out of the city. This change was very, very difficult; it left me staring into the trees and realizing not only the emptiness and loneliness I felt but the ugliness of it all.

Things unraveled quickly, and within two years, so much came to light for me—including ever-increasing lies and deceit, with him always covering up and gaslighting me. Though, at the time, I had no idea that term even existed. I just knew I couldn't live with this stress and dismissive, twisted behavior toward me and the kids. I felt like I was going crazy. One day, I even said to him, "You are sucking the spirit and soul out of my entire being!"

But I never, ever wanted to get divorced. I thought I would do anything to make this work. And I did. I thought that's what people do. We had a therapist, I got my own after a while, and then we went to a retreat and everything seemed wonderful again for a couple of weeks or so. Then he left his phone at home one day. I saw a text. It was so disgusting and vile. It was from what seemed like a sex place or escort service. He came home and went to bed, and I stayed up the entire night online searching the number and places. That's exactly what it was. A massage and escort service.

I think the next day was Christmas Eve. I was leaning over him looking at his phone, and I asked him who these two women's names were. He threw the phone down and responded like I was out of my mind. That was the beginning of the end. There were lies and more lies. I started digging through our things and papers. I found an entire notebook he created outlining my mental incapacity similar to a disease that a family member had. But everything written down was describing him and all the things he had said and done. Wow.

After I spoke to a lawyer, following the first couple of meetings, he told me I was a victim of spousal abuse. I had no idea what he was talking about. Abuse? Victim? Me?

My therapist described my image of our young relationship from my perspective—a beautiful golden statue. But every lie, every hurt, every time he would take a piece of me, year after year, it was like another layer of cement being poured on top. And finally, there was not even a hint of gold to be seen or a vision of the sparkling, conjured image that once stood in my garden.

I have been divorced now for eight years and into the eleventh year of financial abuse, litigation abuse, emotional abuse, and more. What I've suffered at the hands of my ex, his attorney, and the family court is so mind-blowing that there are no words to express what I've experienced and watched others endure—the same and even worse.

I don't consider myself naive or stupid. I just didn't realize that there could be someone posing as a human being, who pretended to love me, who could be so dark and evil and twisted. It's something I have come to understand is likely narcissistic personality disorder. Now, gazing at the emperor with his clothes off, I see everything.

Every day, I think back over the first days I met him. The weeks, the months, and the years that he twisted and manipulated the entire essence of my being. In those first months and years, he wasn't totally like this, of course. But it was deeply embedded in him, and it grew and grew like a cancer. He attempted to bring me to my knees to boost himself up.

I've lost count of how many times I've moved in the last five years with my children, because he owes me and my family hundreds of thousands of dollars. I've sold every piece of jewelry and item that was worth just anything, big or small, to pay rent and buy clothes for the kids. I have spent weeks on the phone with the schools, the psychologists, the college administration—begging for understanding, protection, aid, and money. He hid all our money, "his money" after the divorce, and has kept me in court to keep this battle going. He has not paid child support, alimony, medical expenses, or education costs as ordered. At the very beginning, he threatened to bankrupt and decimate me.

He lives like a multimillionaire with a house, cars, vacation homes, and more. He lives this way because he has hidden money through his business and his family. He has frauded the IRS, forged documents, and hidden money in every way fathomable. And he's made a mockery of the courts by doing it right in front of them. They have enabled him. They have empowered him. They have rewarded him.

Ten years and counting, I'm trying to move on with my life. Many court dates await. Hundreds of thousands are owed to me, my family, and our children. But I'm not alone. Very, very sadly, I am anything but alone. There are thousands and thousands of us.

But the tides are turning. They're turning for me. Knowledge is power, and because of social media, we are all gaining knowledge and we are all coming together. I hope my story reassures those like me that you are not alone—and I hope it warns young women about what to look out for when choosing a mate.

NOTES

We all grew up watching fairy tales and rom-com movies where the man showered his lady with over-the-top romantic gestures. In Disney movies, it's always a prince. So, when women reach adulthood, it's ingrained in our minds that this is normal. This is what happens in the movies all the time, right? So, this must be okay.

It's only through hindsight that Cathy, and many of us, recognized the abuser's manipulative moves for what they were—love bombing. She articulates what so many victims of coercive controllers/narcissistic abusers say: I just didn't realize anyone could be so duplicitous, so evil. The biggest lesson we can learn from her story is to trust our gut and not ignore whispers from the universe. Abusers are quick to explain away any doubts and make us feel like we're crazy. Then we then talk ourselves out of our intuition. It can be a deadly mistake.

The most powerful thing we can do is to learn to love and trust ourselves again—and teach the importance of trusting your gut to our children. That way, they will not follow in our footsteps. Roller coasters are only fun in amusement parks—not in relationships.

— Amy Polacko

THE ABUSER'S PLAYBOOK

Michelle's Story – United States

M y name is Michelle and I want a divorce. These are the very words that initiated my living hell.

Three years ago, I was free of debt, naive, and trusting. Now, with over $300,000 in legal fees and deep in personal debt, I am acutely aware of what can happen in divorce.

Let me make something clear: You don't have free will in these coercively controlling narcissistic relationships. You are being controlled and dominated by someone in all aspects of your life—and it's by someone who's telling you they love you. It's coercive control. The confusion they create is powerful.

I actually thought my husband Jeremy was the "safe option." It was weird though that he didn't tell me that he had been married before until we were engaged and moved together across the country. Then something happened at our wedding that really hurt my feelings, but he didn't care and took the side of his family. Looking back now, that should have been a huge red flag. And even though it would have been embarrassing, I should have walked away.

We moved constantly for Jeremy's job, so mine was second priority and our life was a roller-coaster ride. Sometimes he was super nice and other times he'd yell at me and call me names. We had several children so it wasn't easy to leave. He isolated me from family and limited my friendships.

But one day, I visited a friend out of town and told her how he woke the kids up in the middle of the night to tell them, "Your mother's a whore and a bitch." I'll never forget the look on my friend's face when hearing this and her adamant warning: "You've got to get out of there." It was a mirror of my reality that I had carefully hidden for years.

That's when my mentality shifted. I knew I had to get out but wasn't sure how. Jeremy threatened me, "I will ruin you and take all your money. You will have nothing and live on the street. You won't have the children—your children will hate you. I will destroy your career and destroy anyone who tries to date you." But he said the flip side was if I stayed with him, nothing would happen, and that life would be easy.

At first, I thought these were just empty threats and nothing that he would really act on. But I soon learned he was telling the truth. He had The Abuser's Playbook, and I am certain he had used it before in his prior marriage and relationships.

One important thing I want all women to know is this: I don't care if he never hit you. If he scares you, gets in your face, or threatens you, it's abuse. If he manipulates you, gaslights you, or isolates you, it's abuse.

The reason why I couldn't send Jeremy away is he didn't cross the line. We need to move the line. He'd get in my face, spit, threaten me, pull me places, and lock me in a room—but I didn't have bruises, black eyes, or broken bones so he wasn't arrested. It's time to move the damn line.

I had proof of him locking me in a room and he should have been arrested. But the police couldn't arrest him because coercive control is not illegal in my state—and if I didn't have an incident of physical violence, there was nothing to report. Jeremy was stalking me, following me with a GPS tracker, but somehow the police believed him when he said, "She's abusing me."

In one instance, the police came and took me to their station where I spent an overnight in jail, based on Jeremy's claim that I was on drugs and dangerous to him and the children. My husband waved through the window with a sick smile on his face that said "I told you so" while they carted me away. He also called the station repeatedly that night, asking if he could pick me up.

Every time I tried to leave, he'd call the police and do the same thing. This happened at least six times. The scariest part is they often believed him.

Yes, Jeremy effectively got multiple restraining orders—against me. He did this because I wasn't giving up on wanting a divorce. The message was loud and clear: If you keep pursuing this, I will punish you.

In one instance, he took my kids, offering to lift the order if I dropped the divorce.

If he was so scared for his safety, then why was he showing up at my apartment complex? And why did he request to take the restraining order off so he could attend my mother's funeral? He also invited me to dinner, events, and activities. He begged to drive together to take the kids to summer camp. He definitely had plans: to trap me in circumstances and engineer a story that made me the abuser and him the victim— although it was quite the opposite.

For a long time after knowing I wanted out, I was trying to appease him and keep the peace. I was naive. He would invite me to his place to talk, and I thought we'd be trying to figure out a way to compromise and end this amicably—but it always resulted in him going off the deep end. What gave me power was when I recognized this blind spot I'd had. And that keeping the peace in our relationship was my role and the way I enabled him for over a decade.

A warning to all women out there: Don't look at his words. Look at his actions. From the day you meet.

I exited my home with clothing and what I needed to do my job in May of 2020 and filed for divorce in July of 2020. The day I filed, I received thousands of contacts from him from phone calls, text messages, emails, and knocks on my door. I was not safe. Jeremy told me that divorce was war and that I wasn't going to win. He told me repeatedly that he would ruin me and anyone who helped me. The police couldn't do anything, wouldn't do anything, and even told me that I wouldn't get a restraining order so don't bother.

Words cannot express the amount of trauma—and the effects on my physical and mental health—since this all began. You can't sleep. You wake up and wonder what has hit next—you look at your phone. You know there will be emails and texts abusing and threatening you on a daily basis. Jeremy started charging up my credit cards. He would take large amounts of cash from the joint checking account. He started spending my entire paycheck the minute it hit the checking account, leaving no money for me.

Litigation tactics by Jeremy and his counsel have cost me immensely in legal fees and time away from work. These are bullying tactics that harm me and my children.

Jeremy and his attorney do not participate in good-faith settlement negotiations. We attempted mediation but he refused to negotiate basic terms of a divorce. He had a list of extreme demands for money and assets but would not negotiate.

We write stipulations then revise, add, and amend them with a low success rate. Jeremy has refused to allow me access to my own possessions, including photos of my own children, for over three years.

Two years into the process, he brought in two guardian ad litems (attorneys for the children) to extend the divorce process even further without good reason. The process is invasive and upsetting to the children and meant to only harm me.

Depositions have been scheduled, rescheduled, and equal to eight hours of extreme harassment. These include asking questions about topics not relevant to a divorce proceeding, probing into my personal life, and making detailed inquiries about my work travels and clients.

Recently a parent coordinator (PC) was appointed—a new platform for my ex to verbally assault and abuse me, sending lengthy and derogatory emails to the PC, emails I have to read and pay an expensive attorney to read. In six months, she has made two decisions and read approximately 250 emails (nearly two a day) from Jeremy. Yet no one is calling out the coercion and the way that he is using the system to further abuse me. When he is trying to force a decision in his favor, emails can get to over 100 per day. He even called the PC directly to threaten her and her office staff.

My time in family court could go on for another decade. Without real legislative change across our country, way too many other women will be in my position—continuing to be abused by their domestic partner for years after leaving. Marriage in this country is possession.

The shocking reality is that many women don't have the right to get divorced. I think when you sign a marriage certificate, there should be conditions if you file for divorce. For instance, if a certain period of time goes by and you can't reach a separation agreement, it will be decided for you. Imagine how people would act then. It takes the power away from them. Limit the total number of motions and stipulations, and force the end.

Instead, coercive controllers/narcissistic abusers are allowed to weaponize our court system for their own ends. These individuals know how to go just up to the line—but not get in trouble. It is in the playbook.

After spending hours in jail on bogus charges and ridiculous accusations against me, I decided to testify in my state in support of an abusive litigation bill. It is crucial to give judges the ability to apply consequences to those that use the family court system to destroy lives.

This is just a game to abusers. But this is my life. This is our lives—and our children's lives. We must change the rules and create consequences.

My last message for women is this one: You have to leave. This is not an option. You have to leave for your sanity. To survive.

NOTES

Most victims of coercive controllers/narcissistic abusers are empaths—people who are trusting, empathetic, and kind. Michelle will tell you that was her. And one of her biggest regrets was playing right into her husband's plans by repeatedly meeting with him to "discuss" their divorce civilly and iron things out. She did it to keep him calm. Except, on multiple occasions, he turned the tables and called the police, claiming she had abused him. "If I had only known The Abuser's Playbook," she said, "I would never have done that. But I had no idea." That playbook includes abusers taking an immediate offensive posture on the legal play-ing field—including filing ex parte (emergency) motions for custody and temporary orders of protection and having spouses evicted from the family home, among other things. Their goal: endless litigation to financially and emotion-ally drain, and ultimately defeat, their spouse.

Michelle's story illustrates the point that the majority of women have no idea such things happen—or could happen to them. We often think that we can come to a compromise civilly with these high-conflict types, but this is usually not the case. Often they will use mediation as a tactic to delay divorce proceedings and also to bully their victims. This underscores the motivation for this book: Every single woman needs to be educated about how the family court system can be weaponized against them. We hope they never have to use this knowledge. But if they don't at least know this kind of vindictive war is a possibility, find the right attorney to defend them, and prepare, they could end up like Michelle and others. She is entering year four and still has one simple request for our justice system: I want a divorce.

—Amy Polacko

HELL IN PARADISE

Amber's Story – United States

I met Brendan on the dating app Tinder. Five weeks later, I was pregnant. I was thirty-eight years old, sober, and thriving—ready for a healthy, strong, committed relationship based on trust and respect. I knew I wanted a husband and kids. He was my same age. Tall and good-looking. He drove a luxury car and said he was a real estate agent. Little did I know, in reality, he drove an Uber to make ends meet, lived in a flophouse with his buddies, and had a troubled past that included restraining orders and a string of victims. I probably should have trusted my instincts when, at the close of our first date, I told him "thank you for a nice time" and figured I'd never see him again.

With his piercing blue eyes and a childish grin, he grabbed my hand across the table and insisted we go to dinner. I resisted, but he absolutely would not let me leave. Looking back, I see now this was my first and last chance to get out—but I missed it. So, we went to dinner where he talked about himself the entire time. Afterward, he forcefully kissed me in the parking lot. I was very intentional about my want for an honest and respectful relationship that led to marriage. So much so, I made him promise that we would save sex for at least one month into our relationship.

He forced himself onto me on day 26. Between 12-step recovery work, years of therapy, and an earnestness in breaking generational trauma (stemming from a narcissist mom), I knew I deserved a healthy life free of dysfunction. I was a sober, successful career woman with my own home. Even so, I fell prey to his love bombing and even participated in it, saying "I love you" early on. I was nearing forty and knew my window of opportunity for having a child was closing.

Things happened quickly. I found myself having unprotected sex with someone I truly didn't know but whose intentions seemed to be the same as mine: children and a family as soon as possible. Just a month into our relationship, his controlling behavior was already scaring me. Some of the ways he controlled me in those first weeks were monitoring my whereabouts, getting angry if I didn't text back quickly enough, tracking my activities, saying one thing and doing another, and controlling where I went and who I went with. He even forbade me to go to an ex-boyfriend's funeral. I saw these as red flags and broke up with him via text.

His response was so angry and cutting. His last words? "If you are pregnant, you had better let me know." Pacing my bathroom the next morning, I began to shake as two lines appeared on the pregnancy test. Remembering the soul-crushing abortion I'd had two years before and the promise I made myself that I would never have one again, I knew I was keeping this baby. He came over to get his belongings. I showed him the pregnancy test, and as soon as he saw it, his face softened, eyes filled with tears, and, through sobs, he convinced me to take him back.

He promised change and said we would be a happy family forever. The nightmare of the next nine months was about to begin. At first, I thought I was seeing signs of change; he brought me flowers, got me foods I craved, and was a doting father-to-be, almost in an obsessive way. Then little things became big things. His snoring started to keep me up at night. I retreated to the guest room to get a full night's sleep. He exploded in anger, calling me selfish and inconsiderate. He was jealous of my relationship with my dog and at one point locked her out of the house in a rage. Upon hearing her incessantly barking, I asked him about it, and he acted like he didn't know why she would be barking.

At even the smallest incident, I was called "crazy" and he would mock my childhood. I felt like a prisoner in my own house. One early morning in September, I came to him and quietly said, "Your anger scares me so much. Can we please go talk to a therapist about this?" While sitting in the therapist's office, Brendan was seething with anger, rattling off a laundry list of why everything was my fault. He was spitting the words out: "If there's someone to blame, it's Amber. It's her fault. She's broken. She didn't try hard enough. She's trying to break up our family." When, in actuality, I was just scared of his anger, hoping someone would help.

After forty minutes of Brendan's tirade, the therapist finally got a word in, turned to me and asked, "Amber, how do you feel?" Hands trembling, I mustered up the courage to say, "I'm scared." Aghast, Brendan jumped to his feet and screamed, "Well, if that's how she feels, I'm outta here!" and stormed off. With him gone, the therapist turned to me and locked eyes with mine, saying firmly, "Amber, for the sake of your life and your unborn child's life, run as fast as you can. Get away from this monster and don't look back." I heard him loud and clear, but how was I going to do it? He lived in my house, and I could tell he wasn't going to leave. We drove separate cars to the therapist's office. As I drove away from there, I glanced at myself in the rearview, and the next few months flashed before my eyes.

The thought of living trapped in a house with him and a newborn sounded like hell on earth. With an early December due date, I realized that to be around family for the birth and holidays, I would need to travel soon or not see them at all for the first crucial months. My mind raced with thoughts of the plan I had been forming. I got home that night to him sitting in my living room indignantly. He insisted we call my parents to see if they supported my thoughts of us breaking up. He broke my parents down with his sob story of wanting to keep us together. I remember screaming on speakerphone, "I just want him out of my house."

To my horror, my sweet dad calmly replied, "Amber, for the sake of the baby, give him another chance." I felt defeated. Even my support system wasn't working. We moved to my warm-weather state and lived in my parents' duplex (they lived upstairs, we lived downstairs). We split bills and I gave birth to Mia, the baby I had dreamed of. I threw myself into motherhood and was living on that pink cloud I can only call "newborn bliss." His life consisted of endless hours of playing video games, watching movies, and obsessing over football from the comfort of my parent's old La-Z-Boy recliner. Brendan did all this while making snide remarks about the audacity of my dad charging us (a very reasonable) rent. Within two months, his negative vibe became so intrusive and toxic that I again asked him to go to therapy to try to make this work. During that therapy session, he badmouthed me so brutally the therapist told me to plug my ears. She exclaimed, "I've never seen anger like this in my office," and asked him to leave.

By the time Mia was two months old, I told him again I couldn't handle his anger so I moved upstairs with my parents. At which point they let Brendan know he could stay and pay the whole rent or get his own place. Claiming "there are no good jobs here," he moved back to his home state to "make a living." Over the next two years, I kept up FaceTime calls between him and Mia, and I brought her for regular visits, including visits to his family in another state. He contributed minimally to Mia's financial needs and came to visit her once. It became clear that he still thought we should be together, as a couple, almost acting like we were together. I told him I had moved on and was in a relationship. I created a boundary that we only focus on Mia during our calls and communication. His incessant need to control me forced me to block him. He became enraged, and then the post-separation revenge attacks began. He wrote accusatory, degrading, derogatory emails to any of my friends and family he had met. He also posted horrible things on Venmo, Facebook, and other public-facing sites—even though he knew I had a public profile with my job.

He filed for full custody and sought out mediation. When I described the story and his behaviors to the mediator, she immediately recommended I file a restraining order. My first order for protection was granted through 2023. However, somehow I was tasked with keeping communication open for him and Mia.

One day, I received a call from a number I didn't recognize. It was the call I had been waiting for. It was Brendan's next victim, Kim, whom he also met on Tinder and trapped with a baby (at an age twenty years my junior) within months of meeting. I couldn't believe it. She was on the other end of the line and ready to tell me her whole story and, oh my gosh, it was almost exactly the same as mine.

The best part? She was ready to escape. She said she had witnessed the abuse of my daughter at the hands of Brendan and it shook her to her core—knowing that that would be her and her daughter someday soon if she didn't get out. She told me everything. She told the other side of the story that I already knew had happened. She told me how he abused Mia from the day she started coming to stay with them (the judge had ordered three overnights per week). She told me how Brendan trapped my daughter in her room for five hours, called her a liar, and said he "didn't even want to look at her" because he was so disgusted by her. Kim and I are still in touch and speak daily. We have banded together as a solid protective mom team, ready to fight to end coercive control and child abuse.

Little did we realize just how difficult that would prove to be.

Flash forward to today. I am successful in my career, performing in the top 2 percent of my company, and have been recognized nationally and locally with numerous awards. I am in a five-year relationship with a wonderful man, and we have a sweet, blended family. His children and Mia get along great. Mia goes to a beautiful school and is thriving. (She refuses the court-ordered supervised visits—sits shaking in the car, terrified, not willing to go inside.)

I am often asked to speak to various groups (including schools), and I volunteer on boards in the community and was nominated as a director of my local business organization. I am well liked and respected. After four years in the court system, there has been no ruling on custody—so no end in sight. We had the biggest mound of evidence you could ever imagine, including Kim's eyewitness account of Brendan's abuse (she was willing to testify for us!), chest-cam footage of him blatantly lying to police, pictures of his drug paraphernalia and alcohol abuse, the list goes on.

The judge would not even hear our case, granting my subsequent restraining order but only to protect me, not Mia. I was crushed. I feel some sense of safety, but Brendan continues the post-separation abuse and smear campaign against me. Actually, as I write this, a detective just came to my house. I know this is yet another ploy by Brendan. He has already filed seven false restraining orders against me and my boyfriend, reported fake abuse to child protective services, called detectives and the FBI, and told his made-up stories about me to anyone who will listen.

No one should have to live like this. Will this madness ever end?

NOTES

Most victims of coercive controllers/narcissistic abusers fantasize about being able to talk to their abuser's other targets—so they can validate each other and share information. In a world where it seems so many systems do not believe victims, finding this kindred spirit can be exhilarating and proof that you are not "crazy," as he often purports. But often victims of the same perpetrator never communicate. The abuser uses triangulation expertly, pitting current and ex-partners against each other. It's not uncommon for the coercive controllers/narcissistic abuser to even stipulate in divorce decrees that the spouse they're divorcing cannot contact his past or future partners. In Amber's case, the fact that she is able to forge a relationship with Kim proves to be extremely reassuring and supportive. When this type of united front is possible, it can be a game changer. Of course, before you reach out to your coercive controllers/narcissistic abuser's ex- or current partner, you must be sure it will be received positively.

Otherwise, your abuser could try to twist this communication around and accuse you of harassment.

More and more women are finding comfort—and power—in uniting against abuse. Netflix's popular 2022 documentary The Tinder Swindler *traces the story of alleged international con man Shimon Hayut and the women who say he defrauded them. These alleged victims band together to hunt him down and get investigators involved. Ayleen Charlotte, Cecilie Fjellhøy, and Pernilla Sjohölm teamed up to create a GoFundMe to get the money back they say Hayut took from them. It has raised over 183,000 pounds or 227,000 dollars. On the family court front, Facebook groups serve as a way for women to connect and share their experiences in the hopes of educating and supporting one another—even if they were not victims of the same person. A support network, whoever it may be, is a crucial part of a victim's ability to stay resilient in the face of litigation abuse like that experienced by Amber. If you are in this situation, it is essential to form your personal support team.*

— Amy Polacko

SCORCHED EARTH

Joanne's Story - Australia

Never in a million years could I have imagined the harm my children and I would experience through the family court. As I tried to explain to people what the judge said and how he behaved, or how the lawyers and barristers behaved, they all looked at me as though I was crazy. Honestly, most days, I couldn't believe it myself. I naively believed in justice and that the truth would prevail.

The first words uttered in court by my perpetrator's barrister was "This is another one of THOSE domestic violence cases, Your Honour." I was to discover that this man—the judge—demonstrated nothing that resembled honour. My own attorney's barrister held my affidavit in the air, turning to the perpetrator's gang of family and friends in attendance, and began to read out numerous accounts of the perpetrator raping me over our thirty-year relationship. He read these accounts with sarcasm and laughter dispersed with eye rolls to the audience. The malice and cruelty of my introduction to the family court is seared into my memory, into my body, into my cells.

The judge crossed his arms, threw his head back, and chuckled along, adding head shaking and eye rolls intermittently as though he was joking in the bar with his friend. It was an absolute circus. These cruel men spoke in the same manner as my ex-husband had done to me for years. The misogyny was so very familiar. My perpetrator's barrister then proceeded to lie. Blatant lies about me, and my behavior, that just shocked me. At the conclusion of this torture, I ran to the bathroom and was sick.

I was eighteen when I met Andrew. He was nineteen. He stalked me for many months before I relented and agreed to see him. He was very quick to then ask if I'd be his girlfriend. What followed were all the red flags of which I knew nothing about—the love bombing with flowers, gifts, and dinners. He was very charming and attentive. The early stage was what you'd call a whirlwind romance, and we were inseparable quite quickly. I lost my virginity to him consensually, and then the next morning, I woke to him having sex with me although there was no consent sought or given. This shocked me and I was confused. But I was young and naive—something he counted on. Sexual coercion and forceful sexual acts continued throughout the relationship, much worse towards the end.

It wasn't too long into the relationship when the jealousy started to appear. When we were out, he would often become aggressive, once slamming a drink down on the table and causing the glass to shatter all over me. I locked him out of the bedroom numerous times in fear. One night, he hit me across the face, knocking me flying. I ended the relationship when he hit me but he hoovered me back in. I wanted so badly to believe his apologies and that he would change. He didn't.

I escaped for good in 2018, the week after he terrorized me while driving dangerously with our children in the car. It was a long time coming and the children, now fifteen, twelve, and nine were not surprised. Over the years, I had experienced sexual, physical, psychological, and financial abuse. I had uncovered many longstanding lies in the months prior. But I think the only reason I finally escaped and was strong enough to stay gone was that he said he wanted to see other women and requested me to join him in a threesome. It took the shock of the threat to our lives, and the ever-worsening sexual degradation, for me to summon up the strength to finally be free of him.

Or so I thought.

When I told him the marriage was over, his first words were "you're not getting this house," and he made good on this threat. I sought to quickly separate financially as he was starting to run up debt in our business and in a credit account on which I was the guarantor. He took my name off this account and removed me from our business completely. I tried to advise the bank of the financial abuse and revenge debt and threats he was making, but they did not understand the reality of what he was doing and did nothing to assist me.

His mother secured a lawyer for him about a week after I left him. His family has money and reputation mattered—so saving the family's reputation became imperative. Next to my ex-husband's mother, this lawyer was the cruelest female I've ever had the misfortune of knowing. I could not believe how unprofessional these people were—openly making degrading comments throughout the process. Their lack of integrity was simply incomprehensible.

His bullying became overt in typical victim mentality fashion. He spun a story of me being lazy, a bad mother, and that I was mentally ill and hearing voices. We had been together three decades, yet his enlisted family and friends turned on me too, and I was the subject of gang bullying. They all swallowed its hook, line, and sinker. I was completely oblivious to the manipulation of everyone around me until around ten months after we had separated. I could sympathize with his enablers as I too had fallen for the charm and the lies over and over. I didn't know that I would be betrayed again by some in my own family too. This betrayal by those I relied on for support has broken me. I'm sure breaking me is exactly what he has worked towards.

I sought to retain our home in the settlement. I'd been a stay-at-home mum whilst raising three young children and only worked part time in my career. We had a family business and a home of equal value. We each had a car and that was about the extent of our assets. What should have been an easy 50-50 split became utter hell on earth dragged out over three years. He refused to settle, causing my legal fees to be insurmountable. He told our children that his mother was paying his legal fees. For over a year, my lawyer and I attempted to offer an even split of everything. Andrew kept denying this request, then eventually explained he was no longer using a lawyer and that we could work it out ourselves.

What I didn't realize was that all of this stalling was a tactic. At the same time, Andrew was turning away clients from our business, using the business credit account for his personal use for holidays and other luxuries and was winding the successful business down in order to remove it from our asset pool. After eighteen months of desperately trying to be financially free of him, I found he had created a large tax debt in the business and had used the full limit of the credit account without my consent. Andrew had run up around half a million dollars in post-separation revenge debt. And then, all of a sudden, he was ready to negotiate a settlement. I'm sure it was all part of a larger plan to ensure that I was depleted financially.

As the abuse, stalking, and harms escalated over these eighteen months, the children became less and less willing to see him, which infuriated him. Then came the family court.

With his ducks in a row—the huge debt incurred, the business gone, and him terrorizing our children—his lawyer began her family court assault. My perpetrator was threatening me and using this woman to communicate his intent: I was going to lose the house or be responsible for the debt he had created. If I incurred the debt, I was still going to lose the house because the

Australian Taxation Office would take possession of the home to pay off the debt.

For some reason, Andrew wanted to retain 100 percent of the business even though he had depleted it. I now know that this was a tactic to ensure that it was easy to persuade the court to award him the asset. He was asking for something supposedly invaluable, but of course his intent was to claim the tax refund after we were divorced. Andrew was also seeking sole parental responsibility of the children and sole physical custody. He wanted the children to live with him.

I was working full time for the first six months of family court but then couldn't manage it. The demands required to navigate Andrew's vexatious litigation gave me no choice but to leave my employment and devote all of my time and energy to this nightmare. It was hell enduring the onslaught of harassing threatening emails, stalking, and abusive tactics. It's no wonder I was and still am suffering from post-traumatic stress disorder (PTSD). Eventually, I was forced to self-represent in this circus called family court. The court I was relying on for justice and protection was torturing me. I felt emotionally wrought and dead inside.

After many hearings over the next fifteen months, things went from bad to worse. I couldn't afford legal representation, and, frankly, they were not worth an ounce of my time or money. One lawyer had me consent to selling my home—telling me that my signature did not actually indicate that I would need to sell my home. But that's exactly what my signature indicated. I attempted to explain to the judge that I did not intend to sign an order agreeing to sell my home and that I was ill-advised by my attorney. In the meantime, Andrew was seeking that I be removed from the home within fourteen days. The judge did not turn over the order or show an ounce of compassion. Instead, he ordered me to immediately vacate the property. This is the level of malevolence I endured.

The children and I were forced to remove as much of our personal belongings over the property line as possible, and neighbours, family, and friends all came to help us flee our own home before police came to change the locks. We will never forget the cruelty of these actions. We stayed with family and friends for five months before there was any ability for me to access the settlement funds.

I attended two court-ordered mediations for which his lawyer had not provided full financial disclosure, and the only settlement they would accept was Andrew walking away with all the assets. I paid for two full days of my lawyer attending these pointless mediations. The judge then ordered a two-day trial. I needed a lawyer and a barrister for trial. This cost me $50,000. My lawyer and barrister then turned good cop, bad cop and coerced me into consenting or possibly losing my children. Andrew had consented to giving up sole custody once the house was taken, but my lawyer stated that this judge was very unpredictable and he had threatened us: We had better negotiate or we wouldn't like what he might decide. They told me I'd married an asshole, to get away from him, and that if I went through with the trial, Andrew might not only get all of our assets but he might also get my children.

In the end, I received 4 percent of our assets. Most of my settlement went towards lawyers and legal fees for the trial. With the little leftover, I managed to secure a rental property after five months of couch surfing by offering $20,000 in rent up front.

I had no money to appeal any of the decisions.

The judge ordered that we use Andrew's lawyer's friend as the "family report writer." In Australia, this is the person who is assigned to settle parenting disputes and constitute what is in the best interests of the parties, including the children. This "friend" of Andrew's lawyer ignored all evidence of the years of coercive control and recommended the children be ordered back into 50-50 custody with the perpetrator. This also meant Andrew didn't have to pay any child support.

The judge ordered a property settlement at interim hearings without viewing or testing evidence. He then chose the real estate agent we would use and unilaterally determined the sale price of the home. The names of the buyers were also written into the court order—Andrew's friends! The value depreciated, of course, so I would have less in settlement. Each part of the sale of my home was dictated by the court. It was like I was not even on the mortgage deed. I don't think I will ever be able to wrap my head around the level of corruption.

I wrote to our chief justice about the corruption I had experienced and was told my only option was to file an appeal. The chief justice made it clear: He would not discipline this lower court judge, who was known in the media as "Australia's worst judge."

There is absolutely nowhere to go when there is collusion and corruption. Our rental lease is up for renewal in two months' time. We have been on three six-month leases—our housing situation is unstable. My mental health and well-being, due to the ongoing fear of homelessness and forced poverty, is severely impacted. I receive less than 20 percent of my children's financial needs from the perpetrator. I cover the rest for him. The abuse hasn't ended, and in six years, he has robbed everything from us—family, many friends, our community, our home, the family business, our physical and mental health, and even our car.

The only ones holding him to account are my two older children. They have asked him to seek help for abusive behavior—including violence—before they are willing to spend time with him. My youngest sees his dad for an hour a week, and that is only because it is convenient for his father. I thank God it is not more time than that. I know Andrew will not seek help. I know he is unstable. My children, like I did and many victims do, live in hope. Hope is all you have after being targeted by someone who ends up being the most malevolent person you could ever imagine.

NOTES

Joanne's story, like so many, demonstrates the horrific treatment experienced by victims of abuse in the family court system. Beyond that, her story and others demonstrate that this abuse is not siloed to one country. This institutional betrayal leaches into every continent. There is really only one way to explain it: Patriarchy oppresses and individuals in positions of power are given free rein to exert coercive control over others.

The children had clarity, seeing themselves and Joanne as the victims in this abuse. Research by Lapierre and colleagues (2018) affirmed that even in the face of the further exertion of coercive control in post-separation abuse, the children revealed improved relationships with their mother. The ability to be disengaged from the abusive partner is the road to healing for both adults and children.

The Saunders study (2016) affirms that judges perceive that women make false accusations of abuse, are not believable, and that judges themselves believe in gender inequality. The judge and barrister in Joanne's case mocked her experiences of trauma—sexual violence—in the one place where Joanne was supposed to feel protected. This "unsafety" in the systems is an assured silencing of victims. Judith Herman writes about this in her seminal book Truth and Repair *(2023), highlighting how repair is virtually unattainable when the systems continue to oppress.*

Coercive controllers/narcissistic abusers engage in the practice of "scorched earth," a tactic of abuse to antagonize and intensify the financial abuse using the divorce process as the vehicle to do so (Miller and Smolter 2011). Courts often participate, particularly if one person is the "monied" spouse, having their own money or access to funds, as Joanne's ex had. There is profit for all the "actors" involved in the dark underbelly of family court that some call a circus.

—Dr. C

BLUE WALL OF SILENCE

Gioia's Story - United States

W hen I filed for divorce, I had no clue that the next four years of my life would be more harrowing than the preceding sixteen. My journey into the abyss of coercive control and relentless litigation abuse began in earnest.

My ex-husband and I grew up in the same small town, and our relationship began shortly after high school. While I pursued a college education, he headed straight into a military deployment in Afghanistan. Arthur's upbringing had been fraught with turmoil, marked by the traumatic witnessing of his mother's abuse and his own experiences with manipulation, gaslighting, and custody battles involving his father, who had fled to the West Coast to evade child support. Concurrently, my parents had just gone through a divorce, shattering my world's stability. Amid this emotional turmoil, I found myself ensnared in an intensely passionate relationship.

Initially, Arthur seemed supportive of my aspirations of a college degree, but it didn't take long for this to change. When I had the opportunity to study abroad in Austria, his jealousy and resentment became evident. Arthur accused me of cheating and was upset when he heard male voices in the dormitory. Once I returned, he clung to me incessantly, living vicariously through my college experience, spending most weekdays and every weekend with me. I had no space and no ability to enjoy college living as most young people do—he wouldn't allow it. Interestingly, it wasn't just his need to control that seemed to drive his behavior, but it was his need to gain access to the college life that he was void of. Our relationship gave him access to this experience.

Pressures from both our families pushed us into marrying at a young age. Our disparate work schedules allowed us to maintain the facade of a harmonious relationship but, in hindsight, early signs of control were evident. Arthur's jealousy was the overwhelming problem in our relationship—and I, of course, was the cause of this. I found myself walking on eggshells all the time, worried about his reaction to simple events such as required work-related trips and dinners with colleagues. I was compelled to minimize these experiences and was often rushing home to give him an account for every moment of my day. Arthur liked that I made money but didn't accept the commitment that came along with it. I realize now that not only was my career diminished, but my role as a wife and mother was being diminished simultaneously also.

The boundaries of our roles within the family system began to shift more and more in his favor.

Arthur's imposed pressure on me so that I was carrying the weight of the financial and house management responsibilities. It became an expectation that I needed to adhere to in order to avoid angry outbursts. I invested my entire life savings into the purchase of our family home, only for him to impulsively purchase a race car without consulting me. His justification? "My buddies said if I don't get something now, I never will." When I declined to join him for rides in his new race car, his anger was palpable. The home and the race car were just the beginning of many financial decisions of which I was on the wrong side. Arthur received raises without telling me and avoided working overtime, all to place more pressure on me financially.

Our relationship took a significant turn for the worst with the arrival of our children. I became a mere instrument in his pursuit of an ideal family image, with the weight of parenting unevenly distributed. He argued that the physical risks of his job necessitated prioritizing his sleep over my own. On his days off, when he was in charge of child care, he would text me incessantly by 3 p.m., demanding to know when I'd be home from work.

When my youngest child was born, he made it clear, as he did with our older two children, that it was my job to care for our infant. I had no reprieve and it brought me to a physical breaking point. At my eight-week postpartum checkup, I had endured eight weeks of sleep deprivation—with my doctor nearly admitting me to the hospital and demanding my partner care for our infant to allow me time to sleep. This pattern of behav-

ior never went away. It was apparent that the responsibility was entirely mine to care for the children. Yet
on nights when he was not working, he aimed to be the
"fun dad," with no routines in place and chaos ensu-
ing. Of course, the children were and continue to be
the ones to suffer from this lack of structure.

During all of this, like so many victims and survivors, I would attempt to seek a feeling of normalcy.
I now realize I was seeking any kind of human connection. I felt empty and alone. However, this proved
problematic also. If we were invited to a dinner party
or I opted to host an event, Arthur would become
frustrated and again his jealousy permeated. It was
a competition for him, and he insinuated that I was
neglecting him. Often these events would be sabotaged with conflicts occurring beforehand as I was
readying for the event, such as preparing food, or after
the event with my being reprimanded for the time and
money that the event consumed from us.

Arthur insisted on having cameras in our home to
monitor us during his work shifts. I accommodated
his demands, not understanding that this was his further attempt to control me. I was simply trying to keep
the peace and avoid his fury. I learned early on, any
attempts to cover the cameras or disable them meant I
would have hell to pay with an argument starting right
before bed. I now realize that his "punishment" was to
leave for hockey early in the morning on his child care
days and not return home on time, the intention to
create anxiety because I would be late for work. Arthur
also had rigid expectations concerning our sex life and

demands for regular sex beyond the norm. Declining Arthur's advances led to verbal confrontations before bedtime, preventing sleep—his punishment for me not giving in to his demands.

The final straw came with Arthur's unilateral decision to have a third child, despite my reservations. This decision, made without my consent, rendered intimacy impossible and strained our already precarious relationship further. Shortly after the birth of my third child, a pivotal argument prompted him to suggest, "Let's get a divorce and sell the house." It hadn't even crossed my mind as a possibility, given his previous aversion to divorce, likening it to our parents' failed marriages. This seemingly innocuous statement planted a seed of fear, making me feel more shame. Everything was my fault, or so it seemed—the thought of dealing with a failed marriage and three children on my own seemed insurmountable given my compromised self-worth.

Arthur pushed for the separation, and I began viewing it as a positive step to take some space. But then he changed his mind and issued an ultimatum: remain in the relationship or get out of the house. I chose the latter, as once he planted the seed of an alternative life, one without him and the noose he had around my neck, there was no way of going back. However, I unknowingly set in motion a nightmarish journey that persists today, orchestrated through the abusive tactics of the family court system. This includes labeling our relationship as "high-conflict," rather than seeing coercion and control. I now know research affirms that coercive control intensifies post-separation, known as post-separation abuse.

These four years of post-separation abuse have been marked by relentless false accusations, harassment, an unending cycle of litigation, financial abuse, and worse, the weaponization of my children. The family court's biased guardian ad litem (GAL) scrutinized my full-time work and the necessity of childcare but commended my ex for using his family's help. This GAL also ignored my ex's diagnosis of alcohol abuse disorder and instead granted an investigation on Arthur's false counterclaims that I was the alcoholic. All the while, he was violating my first right of refusal, as detailed in our parenting agreement.

Arthur has filed emergency orders for full custody twice based on contrived stories, costing over $40,000 in legal fees. Thankfully, the family court did not believe his accusations. However, he has found other ways to continually exert power over me, including repeatedly filing for changes to our temporary orders, intentionally reducing his income by over $30,000 annually, thereby forcing me to pay child support and demanding that the family court engage the Department of Revenue to mandate my child support, despite my consistent payments through automatic bank transfer.

As a police officer in our jurisdiction, he has capitalized on his position to intimidate me by engaging his colleagues in his strategies. His campaign of coercive control manifested in various ways, from leaving guns at our marital home to wearing unconcealed firearms during pickups and drop-offs. When I requested the judge's intervention, she refused, and he accused me of threatening him. He has used his buddies on the police force to harass me, with the police at my house over thirty times in two years. The onslaught of intimidation tactics has been relentless, including showing up at one therapist's office in uniform to deliver court orders already received electronically. In total, four therapists have quit.

Arthur went so far as to use the department he formerly worked for as a personal escort service to transport our children, calling the police for any deviation that he deemed "wrong." There has been a constant barrage of messages about needing to adhere to the rules he has created post-separation and the family court's failure to hold him accountable. His reckless behavior extended to our children's safety with him exposing our children to perilous activities, such as climbing a three-story house, riding quads and dirt bikes without safety gear, and taking them to our local bar for American veterans. He encouraged them to fire homemade guns without assessing the risks.

The worst of it all was the physical abuse of our oldest, Jake. Jake had a black eye and bruises after a visit, and even after Jake admitted to the abuse with his therapist on a joint video call, my ex filed a claim against me for Jake's bruises to the Department of Children and Families (DCF). I tried to engage the support of our pediatrician, but her explanation was that her hands were tied if DCF was not substantiating the abuse.

Since 2018, Arthur has been under more than one internal investigation with his employer, the state police, for the ongoing use of his position as a police officer to intimidate me. There has been no accountability, and sadly, the state police only investigate policy violations, so even if there had been accountability, the consequences are minimal. The case was sent to the office of the attorney general; however, our state does not allow protection orders for nonphysical abuse in domestic violence. Restraining and harassment orders have been an option, but my lawyers advise that, similar to the protection order obstacle, the lack of physical evidence would most likely have the request dismissed. After Arthur lied to his employer about having a court order to keep my children outside of our parenting plan, I was given the option to complete a harassment order form but warned that I could not be kept safe from reprisal. I opted to forgo the harassment order form, simply because there was too much at stake. Beyond my safety, I also am cognizant that the lack of accountability only empowers him. Not to mention that if he loses his job, I will be left to financially support him.

Of course, as with all protective mothers, the most heartbreaking part of all is the impact on my children. He told our oldest son that I wasn't in charge of him, encouraging him to assert dominance through physical aggression against me. Arthur portrayed me as "COVID crazy," coercing our children to side with him by consistently disparaging me. He unilaterally signed them up for hockey without my consent, all the while telling them that I didn't support them because I didn't take them to early morning practices six days a week. He even turned our children into spies, sending them to gather information he could manipulate in court.

My oldest, Jake, feels an immense sense of guilt for his physical violence toward me, which I am constantly attempting to ameliorate. He is the golden child in his father's eyes, so he gets the brunt of the gaslighting. Silas, at seven, has felt stuck in the middle, self-blaming and making statements of wanting it (the constant conflict and abuse) all to end. Tessa struggles with vicious separation anxiety and oscillates between adoring me and expressing extreme anger. I can see Arthur is wearing her down, and she is feeling the need to align with him more and more, simply to feel safe. I know all three of them feel betrayed. They have seen their dad's abusive tactics yet know I cannot protect them from him.

NOTES

He was always controlling. But as a police officer, he has been able to use the system itself to further exert this control over Gioia and her children. Gioia has become entrenched in this system that identified her divorce as "high-conflict," all the while her ex has been using his position as a police officer to exert power and control over her. The post-separation abuse, as with most victims of coercive control, has been worse than she could have imagined.

The coercive controller/narcissistic abuser's status in society is state-sanctioned protection for victims—yet he is persistently victimizing everyone in his family. It's no secret the amount of power the police possess. Beyond their "protective" role of being able to arrest as well as carry and use weapons, their simple presence can often be intimidating.

Research affirms that police officers perpetrate domestic abuse at a higher rate than the general public (Sgambelluri 2000). Additionally, there is an evident sense of (reasonable) brotherhood in police forces. A police officer who is also an abuser has the ability to capitalize on this, particularly when he has pathologized his partner (or ex-partner) as problematic. Gioia's abuser is able to continue to intimidate her by using others on the police force to do his dirty work for him. He has been successfully able to engage all of the systems, and all of their arms.

As of this writing, there are six states that have codified coercive control as a form of domestic violence. For Gioia, her state's archaic way of viewing domestic abuse—through the violent incident model—leaves her with no leverage against a police force that engages in patriarchal behaviors, exerting coercion and control over her entire family.

—Dr. C

SPIRITUAL ABUSE

Lucy's Story - United States

He and I met the summer before my freshman year of college in my rural hometown out West. He was a young hedge fund manager who left New York to run his business and get some fresh air. So, he said.

I would later learn that he burned bridges quickly trying to be the biggest fish, so he sought out a smaller pond. He had mastered the self-made man narrative and was the closest thing to God I'd ever come across. I was young and lacking direction when he fixated on me. No one had ever told me I had the potential to be special or that I was capable of living an incredible, grand life. But he opened these exciting doorways of possibility for me that had never crossed my mind and promised to guide me there if I followed his direction. I wanted that fantasy life with him and became willing to do anything to get it. So, we began a vicious eighteen-year cycle of hope, failure, and devastation fueled by my determination to be good enough and someday not disappoint him.

I hadn't developed my own inner monologue when my abuser's will began to narrate my thoughts. I chased his approval, which hinged on me making his life my first priority. I had to give up everything because there wasn't enough of me to please him and have my own life. I quit my college sports team, I transferred universities, I didn't go on vacation with my family, I gave up a dream internship, I didn't study abroad, I stopped drinking, I didn't talk to men, I didn't work on bank holidays or weekends, I commuted long distances, I moved ten times. The list is endless. I convinced myself that what he wanted from me was what I wanted for me so I sacrificed for him ceaselessly. Yet my abuser ignored my dedication to him and often treated me with disgust and cruelty, pushing me away both emotionally and physically if I initiated affection. My desire to please him and avoid his dark moods became a powerful tool for him to control me.

There were times when we were in harmony and my abuser transformed. He could completely change to become charming, funny, playful, and affectionate. During these periods, I felt deserving of the life he promised and would melt into relief. I would convince myself that I had imagined my suffering and the costs to contain his rage. But happy times were always short-lived because my abuser would suddenly pivot and begin manufacturing new plans for himself. I didn't realize that in all other areas of his life, he could only maintain relationships and appearances for a short time before his true character would come out and the situation would detonate.

Four years later, my abuser became restless and didn't like the impact from the great recession on his success plan, so he made a new one. I followed him to the East Coast. A couple years after that, I married him and immediately got pregnant. Then, at twenty-five years old, I gave birth to our first baby. A year later, we moved to the Midwest and had our second baby soon after. We moved neighborhoods and had our third baby. Then my abuser took a new position with three weeks' notice to the West Coast. My family helped me pack our house and his office, move everything into storage, and drive two cars across multiple states so the kids and I could follow him a couple months later. Within a year, we moved back to the East Coast and then moved to a different eastern state.

During these years, I poured every ounce of my mental and physical capacity into nurturing my children and protecting them from the instability. They were mostly okay and rode the tides of change much more gracefully than I did. They were happy and insulated from the insanity, which I attribute to the fact that their father was never around.

At first, I bounced back quickly following each major life change, but by 2015, I was so exhausted that I felt like my body was ripping in half. Any free time I had I slept, but it never felt like enough, with two kids still waking up in the night and the endless mothering of small children required. It was easy for my abuser to ignore my suffering because, all day, every day from before sunrise to after sunset, he was out and about doing whatever he pleased. By neglecting all domestic responsibility, he maneuvered me into a position of isolation, vulnerability, and servitude. I often went into circular patterns of thinking, trying to figure out how to make my situation better for myself and the kids, but would always come back to the same stuck place of having no choices.

I could, however, depend on my abuser to step in and help with the kids when he would parade us all into church every Sunday, despite resistance from all of us. He had become increasingly obsessive about church, boasting about his perfect weekly attendance that spanned over years. Was it guilt? Superstition? Mental illness? I couldn't understand his fanaticism but didn't have the energy to fight it.

So every Sunday, whether it be the East Coast, the West Coast, or on the road, our church attendance was required, until I found myself immersed in a well-disguised orthodox, Southern Baptist, homophobic, patriarchal, evangelical church. I made a couple of friends and was thankful for the social relief, but something was off. The saccharine camouflage began to chip away, and underneath, I discovered a system of controlling, silencing, and surveilling women by the leaders of the church. One sermon explained why God wants wives to submit to and obey their husbands, leaving him to make decisions for the family and granting him complete access to our texts, emails, social media accounts, and bodies. A friend convinced my abuser of the benefits to waking me up in the night as often as needed to resolve festering resentment, real or imagined. My abuser would support and counsel young men who had taken a vow of chastity before marriage, at one point even doing a group "sex fast" in support of their "brothers in Christ."

Via the church, he was able to institutionalize and justify his control and cruelty. The expectation of domestic servitude extended beyond the home into the church community, requiring women to not only meet the demands of their husbands but those of the body of believers as well. And it had to be done joyfully, because women must be pleasant in order to make insecure men feel comfortable.

For years, I denied my selfhood and learned how to slip into the shadows of my abuser's hatred. However, with the framework of the church as validation, my array of life choices narrowed further. My abuser decided what I could wear, what I could watch on TV, who I could spend time with, what music I listened to, and what I could and couldn't do on the Sabbath. He ceaselessly preached about Jesus, God, sin, forgiveness, the Bible, church, etc. and shamed my friends and family for any opinion that clashed with the church's teachings. Teachings they called Truth with a capital *T* and are so true that only a man is capable of imparting onto his family.

I became disgusted with my abuser. On the heels of a conversation in the kitchen that ended with him saying, "If you won't provide for me sexually, I won't provide for you financially," I recoiled from his control and chose to no longer belong to him or anyone else. And just like that, with the blood of Christ coursing through his veins and the holiest men in our New

England city galvanizing his efforts, he accidentally maneuvered his faithful servant of fifteen years over the edge.

In 2020, at the height of quarantine during the global COVID-19 pandemic, I told my abuser that I wanted to get divorced. He reacted with pure hatred and ramped up his abuse. My abuser prevented me from leaving the house for a month, cut off my access to money, weaponized the kids against me, turned my friends against me, and conspired with leaders of the church during daily hours-long phone calls. They were working together to have me institutionalized.

The next month, he ignited a bedtime disagreement between me and my son, manufactured a scene, and crafted a story so egregious that I was taken from my children and home in handcuffs. Having no money and no family nearby, I went to stay with a friend in the area for what I thought was a few days but ended up being five months. Following the arrest, my abuser crafted a narrative from mistakes and shortcomings that had surfaced during my years living under duress and used it to justify his cruelty. He blocked all contact with my children by filing restraining orders and refused to relent unless I would agree to plead guilty to the false charges and go to inpatient psychiatric treatment. There was a complete separation of eight months, with no contact between me and my children as a result of his obstruction, aggressive legal strategies, and court closures from COVID that have lasted for years. After I saw the kids with a court-appointed supervisor for three hours per week, my abuser began to allege abuse by me and the supervisor against my children. I endured weekly three-hour supervised visits for two and a half years.

After the children's visits with me, my abuser would interrogate the kids. He made scheduling my parenting time near impossible. He obstructed everything, causing complete stagnancy. The court then appointed a guardian ad litem; however, my abuser's delay tactics resulted in a two-year wait for the final report. The GAL findings went heavily in my favor, but for the kids, it was too late. All three kids were in shambles and had to be removed from mainstream public school classrooms following incidents of racism, hate speech, self-harm, property destruction, assault, and the need for physical restraints.

The school bought my ex's story and helped him keep me out of the kids' lives by refusing to speak to me, provide info, or allow my involvement, despite the court ordering it. It was the same with the therapists. Other parents would contact me with concerns about my kids, some of whom I had never met. One mom was so alarmed after seeing my youngest son dragged off the playground, kicking and screaming, during field day by four members of the school staff following an incident that she tracked me down and offered to help. Another parent reached out to let me know that my ex was teaching and condoning hate speech that my children began using at school. A neighbor informed me that the police were called because my oldest child was screaming for help repeatedly outside of the house.

The list goes on and on, but despite the effects of my abuser's actions on the kids, I still can't get them back.

I have had no contact with one of my sons for almost three years. The court appointed a "therapeutic coordinator" who has decision-making authority and access to records to get the kids the help they need and ensure reunification between me and my children. She has made progress. The kids are doing much better. I have my youngest son unsupervised almost 50 percent of the time. Most of the litigation is cleared.

However, time keeps passing and my abuser continues to delay, manipulate, and weaponize the kids to maintain separation from me. I have spent $600,000 in legal fees thanks to my parents generously offering me their entire retirement to fight for my kids. But so much time has passed that I wonder if there will be any kids at the end of this. They are quickly approaching adulthood, and there is no end in sight for the divorce. Trial dates are booking over a year out and custody determinations teeter on the success or failure of ongoing reunification efforts. The four-year anniversary of the complete dismantlement of my children and life is right around the corner, and the court can't contain the warpath my abuser continues to march.

I tell my story with the hope that it can demonstrate the devastation that occurs in families when the institutions that were set up to protect the vulnerable are broken. My situation exemplifies the need for change within the family court system and serves as a cautionary tale. Women are equipped with strong intuition that can either be nurtured or silenced. In the fog of youth, promise, and romance, it's easy to ignore our internal warning systems and get swept away. But I swear upon my soul that our bodies know, even if we convince ourselves that fear and butterflies can't coexist. They can, and you can, long for a life with someone dangerous. Nurture your voice and find a way to get strong so they can't dismantle the gifts you have brought into the world. Making ourselves small to accommodate someone's rage does not end well. I had to lose everything to learn that, but that doesn't have to be your story.

My story is better than some. If I had to do it over again, I would. I have amazed myself at what I have been able to accomplish as a free and independent woman. While living with an abuser, I acquired an arsenal of survival skills that have served me well. I'm smart and scrappy. I can read situations and people well. I am tough and self-controlled.

I have met countless women over the last four years who have endured similar situations to mine, who have overcome seemingly insurmountable barriers when faced with the danger of losing their kids to their abuser. I have paid dearly to get out of my marriage, but it can always get worse. I was able to leave in handcuffs and not a body bag. But most of all, I'm free to live a life of my choosing. And for now, that is enough.

NOTES

Lucy really didn't have a choice regarding her required attendance at the churches her ex joined. However, it is important to note that some religious organizations can operate like cults, reinforcing misogynistic treatment of women and justifying abusive behaviors in the name of God. This gives the abuser the ability to harness the power of the church and brainwash the children.

As Lucy points out, it's easy to ignore that gut feeling that something is off. And it's not just ignored by young women "in the fog of youth"—this also happens to midlife women who are looking for a second chance at love.

Another situation so many women find themselves in when they decide to stay home with children is giving up their financial independence. How do women prevent this power dynamic if you want to stay home with your children? Ideally, you want to have a prenuptial (before marriage) or postnuptial (after marriage) agreement that states you receive a salary for your labor that goes into a separate account. This compensates you for giving up your career and chance to advance in your current field or get further education. Postnuptials also address how finances are handled in the event of a divorce; however, they cannot spell out custody arrangements. Whether women have a legal, binding agreement like this or not, it's a good idea to keep your hand in something on the side—maybe part-time work in your field that makes you better equipped to hop back in full time if needed in the future.

— Amy Polacko

FIRST WORLD PROBLEMS

Mary's Story - United States

I t's funny how the brain can convince a person that everything is okay even when a person's gut is screaming "run." I was married for seven years. For five of those years, I truly believed I was living in wedded bliss.

I could not see the insidious covert abuse I was living under. I had a successful career, I was self-sufficient, and I come from a close-knit family. My ex-husband, Dan, portrayed himself as the ideal husband focused on family, values, faith, and our shared dreams.

Soon after we married, we decided to start a family. I had two miscarriages. We decided to try alternate ways to conceive, and I underwent several surgeries and invasive procedures with two years of consecutive in vitro fertilization (IVF) treatment to conceive my son. During these treatments, Dan convinced me that I should quit my job (temporarily) to avoid stress—all in the name of starting our family. He seemed genuinely concerned and I believed him. What I didn't realize is my staying home was the beginning of my bargaining away my access to our bank accounts. His care and concern felt overprotective and, in some ways, admirable. Now I know it was all about giving him more opportunities to control me. Slowly but assuredly, I began to see that if I questioned his motives—my lack of access to money, anything at all—that his temper would flare. I learned quickly that my best strategy was to not rock the boat.

Finally pregnant yet feeling insecure in myself— since opinions I voiced were met with antagonism—I began to experience evidence of more overt control. It was like I was becoming smaller and smaller in our home. Once my son, Emmanuel, was born, Dan's behavior was like Dr. Jekyll and Mr. Hyde. He would go from loving and adoring me as the mother to "his" son and then angry and demeaning in a moment's time. While Dan was at work, he would check in on me— not out of love and concern—but because he was monitoring how many diapers I had changed and how often our son had breastfed. I was required to keep a log. He would force me to stay awake at night and pump breast milk so that we could use bottles. He explained that he wanted to be sure that we were monitoring Emmanuel's nutritional intake so that he would have a strong immune system.

What this basically meant is that I was doing less and less breastfeeding. In hindsight, I can see it was a way to prevent me from doing what I knew was best— breastfeeding and bonding with Emmanuel. Dan even resorted to taking pictures of himself holding my son to his breast almost to show Emmanual latching on to him. I thought I was going crazy. It made no sense to me. Eventually, he also began telling our toddler, "Emmanuel, you came out of Daddy's belly."

Sometimes Dan's care and concern for Emmanuel made me feel selfish for questioning his motives. I must be selfish if I do not want to prioritize our son's nutritional intake, right? Dan was monitoring me through the only credit card I could use, which was solely for household purchases, and also through hidden cameras. I became aware that my phone was set up to upload photos to a shared album so he could see all of my pictures throughout the day while he was at work. Of course, in a normal relationship, I would want my partner to see these pictures. The issue was that I didn't even know it was occurring—it was done without my knowledge. I had no say.

The control continued in other ways too. I was given an allowance of twenty dollars for two months at a time, and I wasn't allowed to go beyond a five-mile radius from our home. Anytime I attempted to bring up how I was feeling controlled and stifled in our home, Dan would tell me that I was controlling. I didn't know what was true any longer.

Eventually, I began to realize that my gut was not wrong. When Emmanuel was two months old, I met with an attorney with the intention of filing for divorce and a restraining order. The attorney told me that because I had never been hit, the court would not see me as at risk and that Dan would automatically be entitled to 50-50 custody because that is the preference of the court. I went home broken—in disbelief. And then

I decided to stay in the marriage. Like so many victims, I feared having my child with the abuser alone versus being in the home to protect my child. I guess one lucky part of this is that Dan worked upward of eighty hours per week and I was the primary caretaker of Emmanuel.

However, Dan knew I was unhappy and the behaviors escalated. He began making false allegations to my family about my behavior. He told them I had postpartum psychosis and post-traumatic stress disorder (PTSD). Of course, we tried marriage counseling. But, as with most abusers, he would walk in holding my hand only to create false stories in session about my behavior. The irony is he was only half wrong. The trauma of living in this relationship has caused me to experience PTSD.

I shouldn't have been surprised when he filed for divorce. Emmanuel was eighteen months old and Dan made it clear to me that he would destroy me because of my disrespect and disobedience to him. Yet, still, there would be a showing of Dr. Jekyll's Mr. Hyde. He would ask me to go on date nights, to perhaps reconcile, and he would behave lovingly and portray hopefulness that we could work out our troubles and stay married.

As my deadline to respond to his divorce filing approached, he convinced me to tell my OBGYN about my mood swings, blaming me and my recent hysterectomy. What I know now is that I was in trauma mode all the time—never feeling safe. My doctor prescribed an antidepressant as a hormonal treatment because hormonal replacement therapy was not an option since I have a family history of cancer. I had a reaction to the medicine and, in the middle of the night, I couldn't breathe. I reached out to Dan for help and he watched me—arms crossed—without a response. It wasn't until I mouthed the words: "MY MOM" that he called 911. I'm sure knowing she was in the guest room was enough to make him realize he couldn't let me die right there and then.

The divorce process began, and Dan's erratic behavior escalated. He refused to leave the home, and I asked my attorney how I could protect myself, my son, and my mother who was living with us. I was told that for courts, nonphysical abuse is not recognized. Since the home was shared, I was told I could not change the bedroom locks. Dan would violate my privacy all the time, walking into the bedroom and banging on doors and walls to startle me in the night. I was living in panic all the time. I began sharing a bed with my mom in the guest room—the only bedroom with a lock. Dan accused us of having a lesbian relationship! Eventually, the only option was to leave the family home.

Dan requested a guardian ad litem (GAL) to determine the best interests of our son. What's so upsetting is that it is obvious that the best interests for our son included more time with me. I am not an abuser— Dan is! For the first year, the GAL's visits were only through Zoom. After a year, she visited my home but never visited Dan's home. She made it clear that I had to accommodate Dan's needs, including waking my twenty-month-old son at 10 p.m. because Dan was available to have "quality" time with his son at that time. Additionally, Dan was being neglectful in his parenting, including not feeding Emmanuel for extended periods of time and allowing him to play in unsafe areas with toxic chemicals around. When I expressed concern to the GAL, I was told I was controlling.

As we neared the temporary time-sharing hearing, Dan called our state's child welfare agency and accused me of hitting Emmanuel a month prior. Child welfare came to our home for an "emergency" investigation and when they found no risk factors, Dan, who was waiting in his car a block away, called them angrily asking why I was not being taken away. A year later, I found out the GAL had reported to child welfare that my mother and I made the relationship between my son and his dad toxic. This again from a person who had not visited my ex's home, nor watched video footage of my ex's at-risk behaviors.

Dan was emboldened and seemed to be reveling in any ability to get me panicked, and the system was continually allowing it. For example, one time he called the police, accusing me of hitting him with my son's pajamas. The police did not believe him but I later saw on the police body camera that they were giving him advice on how to protect himself from me in the future. They played into his narrative or—as I've heard —sometimes the police do this knowing that validating the abuser will calm them down. It's even a safety issue for police.

When my son turned two years old, the 50-50 time-sharing began with custodial exchanges every two days. The GAL recommended my ex and I attend an anger management course and a co-parenting course. The course-accompanied workbook clearly delineated that co-parenting is not an option in cases of domestic abuse. The book also gave developmental age recommendations, which included that young children such as my son should not be away from their primary caretaker for extended periods of time. It was apparent to me that the course facilitators could see that the situation was domestic abuse, albeit absent of physical violence. But they, like the advocates at the domestic violence shelter, were not allowed to speak on my behalf in court and speak to the welfare of my child.

As soon as overnight time-sharing began, my son began to express fear of his father. He would cry and scream "Papa, no!" during Zoom calls, he would hide behind the couch, run to the other side of the house, kick the phone out of my hand, throw it, look away from his dad, and be frantic during the entire call. He started stomping on toys his dad had given him. He would scream and hold on to the door of the car, making it difficult for me to get him into his car seat during exchanges. My attorney and I reported it to the GAL, and she continued to say "I don't know what to make of it." We filed for a social investigator in the hopes that someone with a mental health background could help my son and determine what was going on. This motion was first postponed by the judge because the GAL denied any urgency in making a decision. Eventually, the judge ordered that the GAL be present during the

Zoom calls and record them with a follow-up hearing to occur in three months. Thirty videos later, I was directed that I should not console my son. Yet again, the court ignored my concerns.

Emmanuel began to regress in his behaviors. Potty trained and now fearing the toilet, he began grabbing his crotch and moving it around, saying, "Papa does like this." He would try to lick my neck, kiss me on the lips, sticking his tongue out, and would say "Papa kisses like that." I had an Elmo potty-training flip-book, and there is a picture of a naked baby on the changing table. My son would point—putting his head down toward his own penis—and say, "Papa kisses here." I recorded some of this and showed it in court and was told that Emmanuel probably just had to go to the bathroom. In the meantime, Dan was continually harassing me—coming into my car uninvited among other things. I was told by my attorney that the court would not acknowledge his behavior as harassment and that I would only be seen as dramatic.

In the end, the judge, in so many words, did call me dramatic. He threatened me, stating that the next time I decided to move forward with a concern, I would "have my day in court," and things would take a turn and not in my favor.

This set off an even worse nightmare: Not only had the GAL emboldened Dan but now the judge had. Dan took what he had already settled on for financials off the table. Now he was seeking full custody. Every attorney I consulted with had advised me to settle because judges punish protective parents who are seeking protections from an abuser. I kept being told that Emmanel will speak up when he is old enough and I needed to wait until then. Yet, in the meantime, my child was and still is being abused, and the court has the evidence. Emmanuel tells me he just has to do what his dad says or it will be very "bad" for him when they are alone in his home. And I must sit by silently or risk losing custody entirely to this abuser.

In 2023, while visiting family on a vacation in Latin America, I realized that I was being followed. You ask how I know that it was Dan behind this stalking? Because Dan sent me videos of these "thugs" following me. He will stop at nothing to intimidate me. I went to the local police station and they ordered a protective order for me and my son—deeming us unsafe and calling both my son and I victims of abuse—using the words *coercive control*. How sad is that? I am protected in a Latin American country but not in my own first world one.

NOTES

The GAL in Mary's case, like so many, was paid thousands of dollars to assess the safety of each parent yet made no attempt to investigate the father's home. The GAL dismissed hours of video footage proving the coercive controller/narcissistic abuser was placing their child in harm's way. When Mary brought up this fact to the court and her continual fears about her son's safety, her fears were dismissed. Worse than that, Mary was called dramatic and threatened that the court would "teach her a lesson" if she continued to bring up her concerns. Mary's fight to remain safe and to create safety for her child only resulted in the judge threatening to punish her for an innate instinct every protective parent has. This is the family court—where the abusers are emboldened, court professionals have immunity, and children are left unprotected.

It's no wonder so many mothers suffer from depression and anxiety. We tell victims all the time: Speak up, have agency, let others know how you are treated! Yet when victims of abuse do this, they are often disbelieved, pathologized, or simply seen as "high-conflict" when the only person who is high-conflict is the coercive controller/narcissistic abuser. Abusive behavior takes place repeatedly and continually and as Dr. Stark explained, when multiple reports are made, "many abused women appear in family court, child welfare or health systems carrying pseudo-psychiatric labels that imply they are the problem, not the abuser" (2012, 7).

Mary now recognizes that sounding the alarm for abuse only made her look worse to a court system already biased against mothers and their children. Mary's case, like so many, shows us how protective mothers are silenced for doing what is expected of them—protecting their children.

—Dr. C

THE SLOW DRIP

Emily's Story – United Kingdom

L ike so many of these stories, ours started as a whirlwind fairy tale. We met at university, became immediately connected, and within three months, we had relocated to the other side of the world together. For all intents and purposes, we were living our best lives. We were seeing new places, having wonderful new experiences, meeting new people, and doing things we'd never done before. At least that's how it looked.

Except behind the scenes, the red flags were starting to wave. At home, beyond the front door, Jude began to show a pattern of criticism, invalidation, and gaslighting. It flowed as a slow drip and permeated my psyche. I was slowly becoming conditioned to feel bad about myself, how I kept the house, how I felt, how I thought. I began to think, *I need to think like Jude, because the way he does things is the right way and I just need to* trust *him.* It felt like this was the way everything was supposed to be, that I was being the way I was supposed to be. I ignored my own body's response and knew deep down inside that if I just did as I was supposed to, then everything would be okay. Dependency was setting in, and this was exactly what he had hoped for.

We were never married. I was never quite good enough for this type of commitment. But slowly and assuredly, Jude took over all aspects of my life, including my relationships with friends and family. He planted seeds of doubt: "They didn't really like you" or "They aren't trustworthy." It became more and more challenging to retain the relationships I had built throughout my life. He also began to take over my finances and assured me that my career was not of any value. According to him, I'd never be successful like him, and because of this, he needed to control the finances. He made his views about my career very well-known: It was a "shitty" career and I was worthless.

Then there was a glimmer of light, a promise of commitment and a family: a proposal. This was something I'd waited for. I felt worthy and wanted, a feeling that hadn't been too familiar for me. Six months later, the proposal led to us having a child, and eighteen months later, we welcomed our second.

Becoming a mother changed me, as it does most of us. The love that we have for our children is unexplainable. I loved every moment of being my children's primary caretaker. However, I couldn't understand why Jude seemed to show little interest in our family. I was conditioned to believing every excuse as to why he wasn't able to be with us or help with household chores or parenting. I look back now and recognize that, as with most abusers, the children are simply an object. He even moved out of our bedroom to ensure he would not be bothered with children waking in the night. His need for sleep took precedence.

In the meantime, the pressure was mounting on how I could be a better mother and what I "should" and "should not" be doing. This included how to breastfeed and what I should look like while caring for our children. Jude's standards were insurmountable—and he ensured that I was made aware when I did not meet these standards. By now, I was becoming accustomed to his rules about childcare and the manner that I kept up the home. This was exhausting, and any attempt for self-care was met with accusations of me being selfish. I believed every single allegation that he made and I simply kept trying harder to please him.

The older our children became, the more overt Jude's anger became. He would rage about the children's typical childish behavior. He seemed to resent their growing in their individuality and became more and more aggressive toward them. His enforcement of unattainable rules began to frighten them. I attempted to intervene but was only further gaslit into believing there was something wrong with me. After a year of this, I felt I had no option but to leave. I couldn't bear to watch the children living in such an unsafe environment. When I told Jude of my plans, he told me he would kill himself, and that I had ruined his life.

"You had me over," he would tell me. In other words, I had tricked him. At the same time, he told me that no one would want me and I'd never find anyone like him.

What was missing in his rages was any indication that he had any love for me. I now know that these individuals are incapable of authentically loving and our relationship was predicated on a lie.

However, I remained disillusioned by the belief that if I removed myself from the picture (because, of course, I was the problem) that he would be happy and that we could actually co-parent. This false hope drove me for years. It led to me repeating patterns of behavior from our relationship, believing that my submission was required to keep him happy and that I was better off remaining silent, rather than sharing the children's struggles and their fears.

The children and I slipped silently into the emotional abyss, trying to retain equilibrium in the home and the rage at bay. The threats, intimidation, and guilt-tripping became part of my everyday life. Jude's poisonous narrative was now not just that I was a terrible mother, but that I was selfish and ripped our family apart. Every single action I did was criticized. I felt trapped even though we were no longer living together. How outrageous it was that I would consider taking the children on holiday, how frivolous I was for buying them a toy each for their new bedroom in our new place. According to Jude, the activities and plans I was making for the three of us were negligent and uncaring. This narrative was not only being delivered to me but also to the children, through perceivable innocuous insinuations about me, which served to erode their sense of trust and safety in me as their safe haven. I now know this is exactly what a coercive controller/narcissistic abuser will do—weaponize the children against their one safe parent.

When the children started to display concerning behaviors, acting out and showing signs of significant anxiety, I was conditioned to his gaslighting. I was of course "seeing things wrong." The problem must be me. The turning point came when he attempted to stop me from picking the children up one day, telling me that I couldn't see them.

I dipped a toe in the water and rang the police. This was the start of my journey towards self-advocacy. Sharing my experience with others meant slowly breaking the chains of shame. I was removing the cloak he'd slowly shrouded me in that kept me small, silent, and powerless. Taking that cloak off has been a deeply liberating and empowering but simultaneously distressing and re-traumatising journey. This is because reaching out for support and speaking out has meant coming into contact with the family court system. A system that was introduced to me by him so he could fight for his rights and have his entitlement as a father upheld.

Our journey in the family court arena began in 2019 as we began to navigate custody of our children. Jude's abuse had been documented by child protective services, and he had refused to collaborate about the welfare of our children. I entered the family court arena full of hope and with a belief that justice would be served. Above all, I naively thought that if I told the truth, everything would be okay and that our children would be protected. Family court became an opportunity for Jude to accuse me of abusing my children, an ex-wife scorned and fueled by jealousy. All the while, the reason I left was due to his abusive behavior. Jude's barrister treated me as the abuser that Jude is and convinced the presiding judge that my ex should have more time with the children. A 50-50 arrangement was made with my concerns dismissed.

We've been back to court since this first time. Of course we have! Despite the escalation of his control in the wake of the final judgment, I was able to gain strength. You ask how? Because I became knowledge-able about who he is: He is a coercive controller. He is a narcissistic abuser. I have shifted my mindset from me being the problem to understanding that my ex has a significant pathology. He doesn't know how else to be other than to be vengeful. He's continued to use the same tactics, denigration, deceit, and of course, DARVO—denying his actions, attacking me and our children, and reversing victim and offender. He's con-tinued to control and weaponize our children. It's painful, it's relentless, and it's exhausting, but knowl-edge is power.

NOTES

Emily now knows that Jude continually was imposing his will on her and crossing her boundaries. This "slow drip of coercive control," although hard to see while in the rela-tionship, is something she can see very clearly now. It forti-fied the trauma bond for her as it does for so many victims. Knowing that boundary crossing is a huge red flag and that Jude's continual pattern of diminishing behaviors and rages are signs that a relationship is abusive might have led Emily to escape sooner. These behaviors can be frightening, and as Dr. Ramani Durvasula tells us in her book It's Not You *(2024), narcissistic abusers are challenged in controlling their impulses, especially when they feel provoked, envious, or disempowered. This is a common thread throughout these stories. A victim attempting to hold her boundaries in place, and in some cases attempting to escape, may be contending with a volcano readying to explode.*

Emily tried to tell the family court about Jude's overtly abusive behavior. Jude even had substantiated cases of abuse through the United Kingdom's child welfare system. But none of this mattered. She was treated like a pariah and accused of abusing her children even though there was no proof that she had ever harmed her children. Jude was awarded 50-50 shared parenting time. As Laura Richards, a British criminal behavioral analyst and coercive control expert states, "Abuse is a pattern, a war of attrition that wears a person down . . . Coercive control is the very heart of it" (Nugent 2019).

Emily discloses for us her healing here. She has engaged in radical acceptance—engaged in her own personal power. She knows clearly that the person she once loved and the father of her children is harmful—he is a coercive controller/narcissistic abuser and he will stop at nothing to further harm her and her children. Her radical acceptance includes recognizing that no matter the harms that the abuser has inflicted, institutional betrayal is prevalent. Predicting that the courts will not make decisions based on the best interests of the children and strategizing how to deal with the fallout of these heinous crimes against mothers and children is better than waiting for the system to protect. Accepting the system won't protect is in some ways empowering. It has been empowering for Emily.

—Dr. C

150 ABUSE ALLEGATIONS

Jane's Story – United Kingdom

I met Joe when I was twenty-two and he was thirty-seven years old. We were together for twelve years and married for nine years. We had three children together. I have now been separated/divorced from that relationship longer than I was in it. Unfortunately, my children and I still experience coercion, control, and abuse perpetrated towards us from my ex.

Joe and I worked at the same company and were drawn together. Perhaps now, I realize he was drawn to me. I was young, trusting, and naive. His attention was intense—now I know a telltale sign of abuse. He told me my relaxed attitude to life was a breath of fresh air. He compared me favorably to every woman he'd ever met and made me believe our relationship was ordained by fate. We quickly fell in love, and it seemed that no two people had ever been in love the way we were with each other.

Joe told me he had returned to live home with his mum and dad, which I found out later was not true. I should have seen that as a red flag and stopped right there, but it was hard to see clearly. Joe was quickly talking about us being together forever, and in our second month of dating, he asked me to come to a family portrait photography session. I was surprised by this, and I later realized why his parents also seemed surprised by his inviting me to the portrait sitting: Joe was still with his ex-partner. He had not ended their relationship. No wonder his parents were dumbstruck. I was clueless.

Looking back now, I remember there were lots of red flags. Joe was moody, sometimes completely "in love" and other times cold and aloof. He regularly unloaded on me, ensuring I was clear about all the ways that I did not take care of him and the ways that the world had been unfair to him. Yet there were so many good moments—some call this "breadcrumbing"—the little bits of good that keep us holding on to the potential of how amazing things could be.

Three months into the relationship, I found out that Joe was still living with his partner of thirteen years. I was devastated. He convinced me that their relationship was over but that it was hard for him to leave because she was "crazy" and threatened suicide. I believed him. I now know this is a tactic used by coercive controllers/narcissistic abusers to guilt a victim into doing what they want. Within nine months, we moved in together, and three months later, we married. It was soon after our marriage that the controlling behaviors intensified.

He tried to convince me that I had a particular role to fulfill and that I needed to learn it before starting a family. I tried my best to please him but often it was impossible. I was given a written list of behaviors that I must "correct." I was cut off from family, friends, and the finances, although I worked full time. Joe demanded sex daily and, if I tried to avoid it, he sexually assaulted me. He always excused his behavior, stating that he could not control himself.

I believed he loved me and, as my husband, he was entitled to make demands upon my behavior. I didn't know any better. No one teaches young people about the red flags of an abusive relationship. I acquiesced and supported his portrayal as the king of our home and fulfilled the role of the dutiful wife who didn't speak or think without his approval.

After our second child was born, I felt a shift. I began to question this life I was living. I knew I was a good mother and wife, and I was prepared to complete any task necessary to make my family thrive. I knew that I was emotionally capable of being happier without being run roughshod into the ground by him on a daily basis, and I recognized I had a right to consent to sex. I also began to see what was occurring with my children. They were dutiful to his demands, remaining quiet and often silent so that he would not be "bothered" by them. It was like they were there for him versus his being there for them. He was harsh in his discipline—stating it was up to us to "train" them to behave appropriately. The discipline was shame based: He would put his hands on their little heads, making them sit on the floor and silence them at his demands.

I found ways to distract them and kept them busy with extracurricular activities—long walks, time at the playground, arts and crafts groups. I knew we were safer anywhere except home when he was in the house.

About six months before our third child was born, Joe began working as a director of a national social housing company. This meant he was away two to three nights a week. The space provided clarity for me and helped me see what my life with my children could be without Joe in it regularly. The nights he worked away were spent authentically enjoying my beautiful children, indulging in the bedtime routine with baths and bubbles and stories. I realized I had the power to create this wonderful nurturing environment without having to worry about his moods, crippling criticism, and anxiety at the uncertainty as to how he would present himself to the children.

I began to contemplate my escape but was afraid to do so. Then luck fell in my lap. Joe informed me he was going to the United States for a month to play drums with his band. It was my opportunity to escape. I knew at my core that this was not going to be easy and that staying in the family home was not an option. I could not stay in our family home because I knew Joe would access the property whenever he wanted. So, the day he left, I began packing, and within three weeks, the children and I moved and settled into our new rental.

Joe's rage came as no surprise. From the day he returned to the United Kingdom, he used the family court system to aid his continued control over my life and the lives of my children. From July 2009 to July 2019, we were answerable to three individual sets of proceedings. He made unfounded claims and allegations against me to the children's schools, social care, and in family court. He alleged I was a sex worker, drug user, and thief. He accused me of neglecting our children, including preventing them from receiving appropriate education. Worse, he alleged I physically and sexually abused my children. There were more than 150 allegations made in a twelve-week period. My children were removed from my care by social services, responding to his allegations, only to be returned when there was no evidence to support the claims.

Each time a family court decision was made that Joe didn't agree with, he would appeal the ruling and insist that a higher-level judge review the decision. This meant each set of proceedings was protracted, creating a heavy emotional and financial burden. At one point, Joe was so emboldened that he told a judge that he (the judge) should write an order placing my two younger children into a state care home away from me. Joe explained that he would then have them released from this residential state facility, making the children glad to see their father. Can you imagine the idea of forcing children away from their safe protective parents into residential care so they can be grateful for their release to the man who put them there?

The situation was dire. We were referred to London's Multi-Agency Risk Assessment Conference (MARAC). MARAC is a professional team that assesses high-risk cases of domestic violence and abuse. The four criteria for referring a case to MARAC are: visible high risk, professional judgment, potential escalation, and repeat cases. MARAC gave an order that we be moved to a safe house. Needless to say, the children were petrified to spend custodial time with Joe; however unbelievably, even with this order, I was forced to send them.

It made no sense and I knew I was betraying them. But I was afraid the court system would see me as obstructing his time. My biggest fear was being accused of alienating the children from Joe. I know the courts punish mothers if they believe this is occurring. I couldn't take that risk. I had to pretend to believe my children were safe with him, all the while overwhelmed with fear for their safety. How does a mother send her children to the wolf's den and reconcile it to herself and to her children?

Joe didn't stop the abuse. In 2015, when our youngest son was seven years old, Joe physically assaulted him. I felt I had no choice. I had to fight for the safety of my children knowing full well that it could all backfire on me. I received advice from the Women's Aid Federation of England and refused contact with their dad to protect their safety. This act effectively poured petrol on Joe's rage and escalated his behavior and abuse. Yet again, the family court ruled that Joe's time with the children superseded any trauma he had caused by his actions.

Eventually in 2018, the Children and Family Court Advisory and Support Service (CAFCASS) appointed the children legal counsel of their own. CAFCASS, a United Kingdom program, was created in 2001 to promote the welfare of children and families involved in family court. Their role is to safeguard the children, including giving advice to the court about any applications made, making provisions for children to be represented, and providing support services and advisement in such proceedings.

The proceedings resulted in my being given custody of my two youngest children. My oldest son, George, fourteen at the time, chose to live with his father. When I reflect on it now, it makes sense considering how much "doting" and caretaking the children were conditioned to do for their father throughout their lives. I believe that George felt emotionally responsible for his dad's well-being. I hold out hope that he will gain the strength to escape his dad, but I understand the challenges in this process. When he's ready, I'll be right here waiting for him.

In 2019, the family court recognized Joe as a vexatious litigator. An order was made stating he was not entitled to make any further court applications without evidence. Thank goodness for the peace that followed. It has taken ten years of domestic terrorism and almost £100,000 to reach that decision.

Joe now insists he is the victim of my domestic abuse and that I have alienated my youngest two. I know this is typical of abusive individuals: the DARVO tactic (when abusers deny, attack, reverse victim and offender). For as long as I've known Joe, everything that he has done to me . . . he then accuses me of doing.

The legal fees have made for financial challenges I never could have imagined. I still reside in a rented property since I do not have the money to put a deposit on a home. The sad part is I had a home. It was left to me in inheritance and I sold it to purchase the house Joe and I lived in when we married.

I wish there was a better ending to this story. Although my two youngest children are safe, happy, and thriving in my care, we all miss George and are worried about him. We haven't seen him since 2018.

I hope one day he will feel he can return to all of us. I get it. I know he is trapped, just like we all were. All this heartache and trauma that was perpetrated by my children's father could have been stopped—if the family court had recognized the numerous applications as coercive control. Joe's ability to further exert his abuse onto all of us was sanctioned by the court.

NOTES

Jane, who was ordered into a safe home with her children, was still forced to send her children into the care of their father—someone they feared—all because the court would not acknowledge the coercive controller/narcissistic abuser's tactics. How does this make sense?

Jane's abuser made over 150 allegations of abuse against her, none of which were substantiated because Jane is not an abuser—her ex is. Research affirms that the toll on children with false reports and subsequent investigations is significant, creating physical and psychological manifestations of trauma, including stomachaches and sleep disturbances, never mind the financial burden on the innocent parent and the loss of reputation (Feld, Glock-Molloy, and

Stanton 2021). *The trauma that occurs as a result of the abusive partner's willingness to engage everyone in their oppressive tactics, including child protective services, is unimaginable. To be clear, research affirms that protective mothers are not believed for their own nor their children's abuse—even when there is evidence (Meier et al. 2019), yet we know that the rate of false reporting for protective mothers is less than 2 percent (Bala et al. 2001).*

As is the case with institutional betrayal, the legal system stalls preventing this harm. It's as if abusers need to keep proving they are abusers and simultaneously torturing their victims in order for any chance that they may be held accountable. In Jane's case, the court did finally have enough of Joe's false allegations and labeled him a vexatious litigant. But the harm had been done. And Jane's oldest son, indoctrinated into the role of caretaker for the abuser, left her home to take care of his dad.

Jane's children suffered considerably as so many children do. Yet, as she shares, her two youngest children are healing. Their world is safe and their attachment to Jane, their protective parent, strengthened. However, her oldest is still trapped. Some children cope in this way. The coercive controller/narcissistic abuser relays a victim status— denying any wrongdoing and reversing victim and offender (DARVO), a term created by Dr. Jennifer Freyd (1997). The children, or a child, may feel the need to be a caretaker for the abuser. It becomes their role—an unhealthy one imposed by the abusive parent. Jane hopes that the attachment that she always had with her oldest will lead him back to her. She knows that the attachment can never be entirely broken, and that when he is able to break free, she and her two younger children will be ready and waiting with open arms.

— Dr. C

I'M DROWNING

Gwen's Story - United States

"As survivors of abuse know all too well, victims of our failed systems are not allowed to be angry. You're supposed to be calm, patient, and ask nicely. But you try to stay calm when it's as if someone is holding your head underwater and you're drowning. Try to stay calm when you're witnessing someone you love being harmed. Try to stay calm if, after you were strangled and you find the courage to come forward, you discover that your chances of proving the abuse are now gone." —Angelina Jolie

This struggle is my everyday reality, a landscape rife with disbelief, systemic betrayal, and a glaring gender bias against mothers. It's a relentless battle against the agony of not being heard, the wounds of a system rigged against me, and the searing pain of being unable to shield my own child from harm.

My story begins in 2007 when I made the leap from the East Coast to Spokane, Washington enticed by an exceptional career opportunity. I had settled in well, found an amazing group of friends who became my chosen family, and relished in the offerings of the majestic Pacific Northwest. Yet, as I neared thirty, the familiar chorus from friends and family about settling down and starting a family grew louder. I decided to explore online dating—a seemingly simple choice that would go on to reshape my life in unimaginable ways following a pivotal fall evening in 2007.

Richard stood tall, exuding charm, mystery, and a striking handsomeness—the very embodiment of the traits that rom-com movies, a staple in my upbringing with my mom, had led me to believe I sought in a partner. Our initial date was fun and engaging, leaving me genuinely curious about him. Following the customary exchange of "getting to know you" conversations, as the evening ended, we both expressed an eagerness to meet again.

To my surprise, as I mentioned attending a trendy new church in the area, Richard asked if he could join me the next morning and treat me to brunch afterward. It felt like a dream come true—a man willing to accompany me to church was precisely what I had been hoping to find. Our date was filled with laughter and the sharing of our upbringing and life experiences. Little did I realize, this was merely the beginning of the extensive research and grooming he would continue throughout our relationship and well beyond.

It wasn't long before we started dating exclusively. All my free time was spent with him, my friendships slowly began to fade, yet I had convinced myself this was what I wanted: us against the world. A couple of months passed by. It was New Year's Eve and a great time to reconnect with my friends to celebrate the new year. We had made plans to attend a party downtown and we were all looking forward to it. It was then that little red flags started to creep in. I thought it odd that Richard was suddenly sharing that he didn't feel comfortable around my friends, how they didn't like him, and that all my male friends were trying to sleep with me. As a person who always tries to be inclusive, I found this upsetting, so I prompted a chat with my friends to see if there was something I missed. It was as much a surprise to them as it was me. They confirmed they had no issues with him. I convinced him he was wrong, so we went to the party. And then, what would become his pattern in our relationship, the harassment ensued. He wanted to go home, telling me that my friends were giving him the side-eye, no one was talking to him, and that he felt excluded. This "fun" event was tarnished.

Fast forward a month or two, and we were practically living together. By this point, the little red flags that continued to arise were issues that we had a hard time navigating ourselves. Prior to meeting him, I had started therapy to work through childhood issues stemming from my parents' divorce when I was very young, to work on my self-confidence, and to learn the best way to navigate my career as a woman in corporate America. Richard agreed that having some therapeutic support would be helpful, and we began seeing my therapist together in 2008. While my therapist had a few concerns, she was mostly focused at the fast pace that we were moving along in our relationship. I could not see the slow erosion of my autonomy and neither could the therapist. Part of this may have been because awareness about narcissistic abuse and coercive control was not yet part of our vernacular. In retrospect, I see how I didn't disclose some of my concerns, such as how quickly our engagement came (by month seven) and I took responsibility for any of our problems, with Richard sitting idly by taking no responsibility. I knew we had our issues but felt that love could conquer all, and that if we both remained committed to working on things, we'd get through it.

Shortly after our engagement, in the summer of 2008, we decided to return to the East Coast to be closer to friends and family. We chose to relocate back to Virginia where I had previously lived, since I had maintained a strong friend network there and it was conveniently located in the middle between my family in Connecticut and his family in Florida. We planned that we would have all our personal belongings packed up in a shipping container making its way across the country to meet us in Virginia, including my vehicle. We used his vehicle to drive cross-country making stops along the way. I had no idea that this would put me at Richard's mercy.

While driving through Yosemite National Park, we got into a major argument, about what I still can't recall. While stuck in summer traffic and construction trying to come off the mountain, it was a situation where I had no escape. Finally, off the mountain, Richard drove me directly to the nearest airport. I couldn't have predicted his fury. He forced me out of the vehicle, leaving me to fend for myself with two cats in tow, and a suitcase. I was disoriented from the whole explosion. I had no idea how to navigate from there since I didn't even know where we were. I was in disbelief that he would do this to me. Overwhelmed and evidently lacking in self-worth, I managed to beg Richard to allow me back in the car but only if I promised to not talk for the remainder of the drive to Virginia. In hindsight, so much of this experience reminds me of Gabby Petito's story—like Gabby, I just wasn't aware of what was happening and continually blamed myself.

Once settled in Virginia, we began establishing our life: buying a house, starting new jobs, and welcoming a pregnancy. Yet, amid these changes, a troubling pattern emerged. Richard gradually exerted control, scrutinizing and disapproving of my long-term friends, discrediting their significance. Even my participation in a volleyball tournament, something I had done for years, was met with criticism, suggesting my time should align solely with our mutual interests. Over time, my world shrank, constrained by his control. He convinced me that combining our finances made the most sense, given he was savvier than me with finances. Richard dictated my clothing choices, social interactions, what I ate, whether I worked out or not, who I could talk to at work, and more, until it was just the two of us, isolated and under his control. His power and control over me were suffocating, despite the six therapists we visited to help us "fix" us. I now know that there was no fixing us—that he has the need to control others—and he was controlling me. At this point, I was six months pregnant.

The idea of leaving began to enter my mind and, even though I knew that was the right thing to do, I was terrified and I had no idea if I could manage single parenting and my career on my own. After a big fight, I broke off our engagement, gave him his ring back, and asked if we could just take a step back, as our relationship had catapulted into so many major life events at once that it was stressing us both out. Little did I know, this was a triggering event that would reopen abandonment wounds he experienced as a child with his father. There was no going back, no matter how hard I worked to repair the relationship or express my love and commitment. My intent to take space was a threat to Richard.

The situation escalated two months later during yet another explosive argument, the cause of which seemed elusive. Seeking a moment of peace and space to process, I attempted to retreat to our bedroom. At eight months pregnant, I simply needed a break from the conflict. However, my attempt to disengage was met with Richard's demand for the conversation to continue, accompanied by yelling and demeaning behavior. Desperate for a moment of calm, I locked myself in the bedroom, seeking time to collect my thoughts and respond in a healthier manner. Instead of respecting my need for space, he aggressively demanded entry. When I pleaded for him to stop and allow me the mental space to think, he resorted to violent measures, kicking down the door with such force that it shattered the hinges from the doorframe. Richard aggressively came toward me and positioned himself over me in a way that I was preparing for him to hit me, with my arm raised to protect my face from the blow. A reaction he reveled in. In that moment, a wave of recognition and also embarrassment washed over me. The grim reality—I was experiencing domestic abuse. Yet the thought of involving the authorities or confiding in anyone filled me with shame. The prospect of police cars arriving, the neighbors witnessing such a scene, and worse, the unknown repercussions once they all departed were all too overwhelming to contemplate.

But it was too late. Richard was scorned by my unhappiness and, following this abusive incident, it became a frequent occurrence for him to go missing on weekends, citing camping trips in other states. Approaching my due date, this left me feeling anxious, fearing I might go into labor without him present, despite knowing his presence would add stress to the situation. Instead of relishing the space created by his absence over the weekends, I found myself reaching out to his friends and family through texts or calls, seeking information on his whereabouts. Strangely, this made me appear as the anxious one, seeking his location when I was nine months pregnant— exactly as Richard intended. Little did I realize that this was yet another pattern I would come to endure repeatedly.

Following our son's birth, Richard adamantly criticized every action I took concerning our child. According to him, I couldn't bathe or diaper our son correctly, and I was forbidden from comforting him when he cried at bedtime. Even my mother, who came to assist during the first two weeks after the birth, was

made to feel unwelcome and incapable of doing anything right.

When our son was four months old, I unexpectedly
contracted mononucleosis while breastfeeding and
had to take antibiotics. Consequently, my milk supply began to dwindle despite all my efforts. Instead of
offering support, Richard shamed me, alleging that I
hadn't done enough for our son and accused me of giving up on breastfeeding prematurely.

Moreover, Richard went so far as to accuse me of
infidelity, claiming that my mono diagnosis was the
result of cheating on him. He believed that he contracted mono from me because I must have been
cheating on him.

During this period, I resumed working, and we
found a remarkable in-home daycare run by a warm,
caring, and supportive family. However, a troubling
pattern emerged when Richard would drop off or pick
up our son. He began surreptitiously sneaking into
the provider's home, stealthily making his way downstairs where she conducted the daycare, all in a bid to
catch her neglecting our son. This was far from the
truth. She was exceptional, and our son adored being
with her and her family.

Richard's unwarranted suspicions became such an
issue that the daycare provider demanded a meeting
to address the situation, expressing a desire to termi-
nate our arrangement. I pleaded with her for another
chance, promising to handle most of the drop-offs and
pickups, and Richard agreed to announce his arrival
more openly. However, the habit of sneaking up on

people became a recurring trend, one that I unfortunately became all too familiar with and, distressingly, now see mirrored in our son's behavior.

A year later, we made the choice to move back to Washington from Virginia, hoping it might salvage our relationship for the sake of our son. Despite this effort, we lived together for four months, but the situation deteriorated rapidly. The psychological abuse, including verbal assaults, reached unbearable levels, prompting my decision to leave. I now know that this is all coercive control— the abuser's goal to diminish the victim using various strategies to do so. I had no idea that the end was nowhere in sight and that his abuse would only intensify.

The atmosphere grew so toxic and unsafe that I felt compelled to sleep with a pocket knife under my pillow out of fear for my safety. There was an overwhelming sense of dread every time I turned my back to him in bed, fearing something might happen while I slept. Unbeknownst to me during our time living together, he began recording me while I slept. This covert act followed heated arguments where he would provoke me and then record my reactions. His demeanor would shift to a calm and supportive one, creating a distorted narrative. Twelve years later, I learned of these recordings and a YouTube channel where he had posted them, as he attempted to exploit them in court. He falsely claimed my sleeping patterns and alleged "erratic behavior" as signs of neglect and depression, none of which held any truth.

Following our separation, we established a fair 50-50 parenting arrangement for our one-year-old son through a mediated parenting plan. Over the next decade, our co-parenting was mostly smooth, with me readily shouldering extra responsibilities to facilitate his freedom and flexibility, especially regarding his travel. However, the turning point arrived in 2018. He had been romantically involved with a woman from Vancouver while residing in Washington; their relationship had its ups and downs for a few years before she relocated to Vancouver. When I declined to move there so that he could live with his girlfriend while having our son nearby, everything spiraled out of control.

My refusal to uproot our lives triggered a chain of events, marking the onset of his increasingly aggressive behavior over the subsequent five years and continuing. We invested considerable time and money in mediation sessions, trying to craft a finalized parenting plan for submission to the court. Yet, just before our last mediation, he unexpectedly served me legal papers, seeking full custody. That heart-sinking moment was the beginning of my traumatic journey through the family court system.

Between 2018 and 2023, I navigated a tumultuous legal journey involving eight lawyers, two judges, and five commissioners. This included enduring a prolonged two-and-a-half-year forensic parenting evaluation accompanied by extensive psychological assessments, a guardian ad litem investigation, and evaluations of my child's mental health. In addition, there were numerous reports made to child protective services and the police, a forensic fraud investigation, and sessions with a reunification therapist. No one could see his coercive and controlling behaviors— or they just chose to ignore what he was doing. All the while virtually every provider was a puppet to his harmful antics.

Throughout this time, I underwent over forty-five hearings and endured a grueling six-day trial. To bolster my case, I enlisted the expertise of seven witnesses who shed light on coercive control, illustrating its relevance to my situation and its alignment with Washington state's new coercive control law. The toll was not only emotional; it has cost a staggering $300,000 from my retirement savings, so far.

This prolonged legal battle highlights the immense hurdles, both personal and financial, I encountered while striving for justice and ensuring the safety of both my child and myself. It's a process that is anticipated to endure until my son reaches an age where he is no longer under the jurisdiction of the system.

Following the trial, the judge presiding over our case, who lacked training in coercive control (what we now know as the foundation of domestic abuse), noted ours as having the largest case file in our county. To those well-versed in domestic abuse, such a voluminous case file is a clear marker of domestic abuse. However, in the eyes of family court professionals, this is often labeled as "high-conflict," implying equal participation from both parties in the conflict.

You might assume that such comprehensive measures would ensure justice and allow me to protect my now fourteen-year-old son from continued harm. Regrettably, that's not the case.

I could elaborate on the distressing experiences during my trial, like discovering my attorney was drinking during the proceedings. When I requested a mistrial, the judge reassured me, claiming everything was in order, and urged me to continue. I could recount the countless hours spent at my lawyer's office until the early hours, as she was unprepared—her staff had quit upon learning about her drinking. Sadly, such scenarios are all too familiar for protective mothers navigating the chaos of family court.

Furthermore, I could delve into the prolonged ordeal with the forensic parenting evaluator, who took an excessive two and a half years to conclude an investigation that typically spans three to six months. To my shock, this evaluator testified on behalf of my ex, despite being out of touch with the case for over a year. Her ignorance of his escalating patterns of behavior, and manipulating my son against me, was evident. Despite our efforts to challenge her understanding of coercive control, the judge inexplicably deemed her credible. I often wonder if she did understand the concept yet was choosing to ignore the abuse.

If she had shown attentiveness to the testimony provided by my son and me, accepted the proposal to speak with my domestic violence advocates, meticulously reviewed the evidence she requested, and possessed the expertise to identify coercive and controlling behaviors, the outcome might have taken a radically different turn. I strongly believe that had these critical steps been taken, the fracture in my once close and bonded relationship with my son, which unexpectedly unraveled in late 2021, might have been averted. It pains me to imagine how different things could have been, preserving the wonderful relationship I once had with my son.

However, instead of considering these vital aspects, this forensic evaluator chose to align herself with the framework that often promotes parental alienation. Revising her language, she labeled my behavior as "maladaptive gatekeeping," which essentially aligns with the concept of parental alienation. This can be a mother's worst nightmare, with research indicating that when mothers report abuse, fathers frequently pursue full custody and assert claims of alienation. When courts credit these alienation claims, mothers lose custody 73 percent of the time (Meier et al. 2019). I was trying to protect my child, yet was punished for doing so. The evaluator implemented this alienation ideology—my son having unsupervised custodial time with our abuser.

It's deeply disheartening that despite the compelling and extensive testimonies from globally recognized and respected experts on coercive control, spanning over eight hours with numerous exhibits of evidence illustrating the existence even twelve years post-relationship, the judge chose to dismiss all evidence. Shockingly, some critical evidence wasn't even allowed to be admitted. Additionally, the judge disregarded recommendations from all experts, including the guardian ad litem's advice indicating the necessity for my son to distance himself from the "unhealthy enmeshment" with his father. In addition to dismissing critical evidence, the judge also chose to overlook the findings from the forensic fraud investigation. This investigation conclusively revealed that my ex had misled the court about his income, concealed assets, and engaged in multiple fraudulent activities. Despite these irrefutable findings, the judge opted to disregard this crucial information and ordered me to pay Richard child support.

Contrary to the evidence and expert opinions, the judge awarded full custody to Richard, drastically reducing my parenting time from the previously shared 50-50 arrangement maintained for thirteen years to mere weekends and limited hours every other week. The judge emphasized the importance of Richard's support for reunification therapy, aiming to restore the 50-50 arrangement promptly.

However, since then, Richard has predictably obstructed any attempts at reunification therapy, refusing to encourage our son's relationship with me. The consequences have been unequivocally damaging to my son, leaving him in a state of harm that I fear might have lasting repercussions, possibly irreparable.

The daily anguish is unbearable as I grapple with the heart-wrenching reality that my only child, my entire world, has been subjected to severe manipulation, leading him to believe I am the one at fault.

He now perceives our shared experiences, cherished vacations, and countless joyous moments as nonexistent, labeling them as fabrications. He holds onto unfounded accusations of my deceit, unable to articulate what those supposed lies entail. The years of carefree childhood memories spent outdoors with friends, the laughter and warmth shared during those times, are now rewritten as nonexistent events. False allegations about me tarnishing his childhood haunt our relationship.

The repercussions of his estrangement extend beyond our immediate bond. He has distanced himself significantly from every person connected to me, viewing them as adversaries, despite their unwavering love and support for him. This weaponization of my son against me has led to a seismic impact, severing ties with lifelong family friends, devoted grandparents, aunts, uncles, cousins, neighbors, therapists, teachers, and anyone who has extended a helping hand or shown him support. The only support network available to him comprises individuals aligned with Richard's perspective, chosen and approved by Richard himself.

My deepest fear is that he may not have the chance to say goodbye to my mother before she passes. She has been his most ardent supporter, showering him with unconditional love from the moment she learned of his existence. The thought of their bond being forever severed due to this devastating situation is too much to bear.

My path to healing from the trauma inflicted by family court, systemic biases, gender discrimination, and the profound betrayal I've endured may never see an endpoint. My therapy sessions are a constant journey of processing these wounds, navigating through a lifelong journey of pain and recovery. The loss of my son leaves me constantly grappling with an enduring sense of grief and sorrow.

Every significant milestone, from holidays to missed school events, and all those pivotal moments like first girlfriends, first kisses, birthdays, and the upcoming milestones of obtaining his driver's license or choosing a path after high school, represents a poignant loss that can never be reclaimed. Each passing day demands an ongoing commitment to self-education, diving into books, podcasts, absorbing insights from experts, and actively engaging in my healing process. I strive to hold on to any semblance of hope that someday my son will challenge the narrative he's been led to believe, start to think independently, and question the memories imposed upon him. My ultimate aspiration is for him to grow into a confident, loving individual who stands by his truth and embraces his loving nature. Despite the overwhelming challenges, I refuse to let my thoughts dwell on any outcome other than this hopeful vision for his future.

There are those close to me who struggle to understand why I continue in holding on to hope. Being his mother means more than just sharing an unbreakable biological bond. It's an inherent responsibility as a parent to safeguard him from harm and adversity, to persist in fighting for his well-being until I've exhausted every possible avenue.

Through my experiences, I've learned that the day will come when his father's facade crumbles. When that moment arrives, it will undoubtedly be devastating for my son. However, I'm committed to being there, steadfast, forgiving, and prepared to support him unconditionally through this difficult time. I'll stand by his side, guiding him along his healing journey, steering him away from the abuse and coercive control enforced by unjust family court orders.

NOTES

Gwen, like so many, missed the red flags of an abusive relationship. She wanted to believe that the coercive controller/narcissistic abuser could change—that he was a good partner and parent. The horrors that she found out later— his recording her while she slept and diminishing her role as a mother since day one—well, completely unfathomable. His intent all along was to fracture her child's attachment to her.

Like her faith in her husband, Gwen placed faith in the court system, convinced that there was no way that Richard's abusive behavior could be denied. What she learned, like every other story in this book, is that the system is rigged, complicit in emboldening the coercive controller/narcissistic abuser and oftentimes collaborating in exerting control over adult victims and their children. Institutional betrayal is the reality for so many.

Seeing her son's experiences through the lens of coercive control allows for Gwen to understand his entrapment—just like her own. Gwen now realizes that her son has been living the life of a soldier aligned with his general. Like soldiers, her child has no choice but to obey. Jennifer Freyd further explains that when a parent who is offending degrades what is a fundamental part of a child's development, their relationship with their protective parent (targeted parent), the child may need to disassociate from the trauma—simply because their survival, emotionally or otherwise, depends upon it (1997). Thus, the child maintains a commitment to the relationship with the parent who has been abusive (Nicholson and Lutz 2017).

It is a malicious fracturing of attachment to the protective parent and harmful to the child's developing brain. Research affirms that this is all too common, and that "62 percent of intimate partner violence survivors reported that their abuser 'tried to turn the child against them'" (Clements et al. 2022). Experts agree that protective mothers (versus fathers) suffer this at greater rates (Dalgarno et al. 2023). The term CAMS—(Abusers') Child and Mother Sabotage—is being espoused as a preferable term for how perpetrator fathers intentionally sabotage the child-mother connection and to explain this phenomenon.

It may take a great deal of time and space for children to gain clarity. This may occur when we have no way to protect our children and/or we are no longer the buffer. This is when the child may feel the wrath of the abuser firsthand. When a child disobeys, or simply does not do as well in a sport or other activity or reaches out to their protective parent, the abuser may begin to show his true colors. Just like with the adult victim, the more that the child experiences the abusive behavior and has opportunities to interact with an outside world that feels differently than the world inside the home with the abuser, the less the child's ability to disassociate. Slowly, yet assuredly, we must believe that children begin to see that the abusive parent does not love without conditions and does not allow the child the freedom to be who they truly are —to be authentic.

Holding out hope that a child finds their path to freedom, away from the abuser and back to the loving arms of their protective mother, is a burden no mother should ever have to endure. Yet this is what Gwen is left to hope for.

—Dr. C

THE CHOICELESS CHOICE

Zoe's Story – United States

I n 2018, during my internship at a local domestic violence advocacy center, I began to realize I was in a toxic and controlling relationship with my partner. At the time, my oldest child, who has a different father, was struggling with self-harm, depression, and anxiety, while my two youngest children, fathered by Luis, also were showing signs of distress. Engaged in therapy to address codependency, I confronted Luis' substance abuse issues, including heavy drinking, opioid use, marijuana consumption, and infidelity. It didn't go well and I realized I needed to leave.

As with most victims of domestic abuse, as soon as I began asserting myself and attempting to establish healthy boundaries, Luis' behavior escalated, the physical violence and mind games became unbearable—all because I had initiated steps to leave the relationship. Thankfully, I had the support of my colleagues and my therapist, but I had no idea what I was in for. I know victims-survivors always ask: How could the abuse get worse outside of the relationship than what was experienced in the relationship? It was like he was holding my head underwater. I couldn't breathe. I was worried about my safety and overwhelmed with the fact that my two youngest children only imagined their father as the "hero" dad.

Concerned about custody battles, given that two of the three children are biologically his, I sought legal counsel recommended by the advocacy center. Despite a reduced retainer fee, the financial strain was significant. The attorney advised me to leave with the children to avoid accusations of abandonment, emphasizing our shared custody arrangement. I secured an apartment in the county, funded by a credit card, intending to work and pay off the debt while pursuing full-time counseling employment. Despite signing the lease in August, fear and duress delayed my departure until November, as the abuse persisted. I know this is the case for many victims-survivors. Delaying the escape often feels safer.

The realization of the exorbitant costs associated with a custody battle dawned on me gradually. Settling into the apartment and establishing a stable routine for the children was disrupted by the onset of the pandemic. Our 50-50 shared custody agreement, drafted by his attorney without input from mine, proved disadvantageous in hindsight.

My attempts to prioritize the children's well-being were thwarted by Luis' opposition to any therapeutic interventions, despite these interventions stipulated in the custody agreement. The pandemic made everything worse, with the challenges of homeschooling and lockdown exacerbating my children's distress. My oldest, Dylan, was suffering significantly, as was evident by his pattern of self-harming behaviors. He severed contact with his stepfather five years ago because he knew that his trauma was from the abusive behavior in our home. He thanked me for escaping the abusive relationship, yet he still continues to suffer.

During my healing, I realized that I had minimized sexualized behavior with my children. I realized that Luis was sexually abusing them. Amid the escape, I felt the courage to disclose this to my therapist. This led to two child and youth Services (CYS) investigations. Mandated to report as a therapist myself, I attempted to file for a Protection from Abuse (PFA) order. However, the failure of our CYS—since the allegations were unsubstantiated, the police didn't follow through, and advocates at the courthouse disempowered me—made me realize that legal action might be a moot point. Of course, all this did was embolden Luis to punish me for making such accusations. The most egregious part of all this has been my inability to protect my children from their abusive father.

Despite my attorney's reluctance to proceed, I filed for full custody, as any protective parent would. Although psychological evaluations were ordered by the court, they were not conducted due to financial constraints. Luis requested the judge meet with our daughter in the judge's chambers alone. Despite my objection, the judge allowed it and ordered therapy between myself and my daughter to work out our issues separate from Luis. At first glance, this does not feel like a horrible order since everyone knows most abusers sabotage therapy. However, this was because Luis had convinced my daughter, Genevieve, that I was the problem, and she relayed this to the judge. It didn't matter either way, since Luis' coercive control over our daughter impeded progress. She refused to cooperate with therapy and aligned with him.

As the court hearing for full custody approached, I could see my children unraveling. I feared Luis might be able to have them fully align and that I would lose custodial time. I knew he was exerting power over them and that it was because of this impending hearing. Abusers will do these things—ensure the children are dysregulated all for the purpose of sending home a message to the protective parent: "back off." Protecting my children felt futile. And then under pressure from my attorney, I withdrew my petition for full custody. The subsequent settlement negotiations left me financially drained, with mounting legal fees and no resolution in sight.

Post-hearing, Luis' tumultuous relationship with his new girlfriend further exposed the children to conflict. It was proof that I was never wrong about what I had been feeling in my gut: Luis was and always will be an abuser. However, it's not over. And with dwindling resources and continued violations of court orders, I find myself trapped in a cycle of legal battles and emotional turmoil, questioning the efficacy of further legal action.

Recently, my teenage daughter's alarming self-harm threats prompted school intervention. Despite my efforts to engage proper support, Luis intervened and sabotaged this support, and for all intents and purposes, silenced my daughter's cries for help. Luis fabricated stories to discredit me and accompanied my daughter to an emergency appointment with the pediatrician to address Genevieve's self-harm. The pediatrician virtually ignored my disclosures of the long-standing abuse, aligning with Luis. My daughter's self-harm was minimized without any regard for follow-up care or interventions. This ordeal, like so many others, exposes the system's failure to address domestic violence.

NOTES

Zoe's children are exhibiting anxiety, depression, and self-harm. Her ability to prevent this is in no way supported by the family court system, with even her family doctor aligned with the coercive controller/narcissistic abuser. It's evident who holds the cards in these situations—and children become commodities to be exchanged. As Joh-Carnella and colleagues' research asserts (2023), healthcare providers are well positioned to report child maltreatment but often feel ill-equipped in reporting and discomfort in doing so.

Zoe knew that her worst fears were true—that her children were being sexually abused—yet she had to make a choice between holding their father accountable and fearing that he would gain more custodial time, or worse, she would lose custody. These are the decisions of mothers everywhere and here, in the underbelly of family court, where a protective mother's concerns about the safety of her children are diminished or entirely dismissed. It's a choiceless choice.

Not all coercive controllers are pedophiles, but all coercive controllers do use grooming tactics to harm their victims. These grooming tactics are virtually the same as the grooming tactics of pedophiles—minus the sexual engagement. Children in these situations suffering coercive control, often have a difficult time reconciling their abusive parent as an abuser. The idea of a loving parent is incongruent with the idea that one's parent is aggressive and violent. As Jennifer Freyd and Pamela Birrell state in their book, Blind to Betrayal, "unawareness is a powerful survival technique, when information is too dangerous to know" (2013, x).

—Dr. C

RESEARCH MEANS NOTHING

Faith's Story - Canada

My ex and I were high school sweethearts. Compared to my own family, Gerry and his family seemed flawless. I was excited to be with what I perceived to be a stable family and good man for a partner. Some women I know have more covert abusers in their home, and the abuse becomes more overt when the abuser recognizes they may have intent to escape. Like many of these women's experiences, I experienced Gerry's covert abuse from the get go—but he was also overtly abusive almost immediately. I learned early on that dealing with the subtle abuse was better than dealing with what would ultimately come next—his rages of verbal assaults and intimidation were often the worst.

Gerry's coercion and control were all encompassing in the household and intensified with the births of each of our children. It's almost like he couldn't handle one more thing on his plate and the children were a nuisance to him. Yet they also served another purpose: an opportunity for him to gain more weapons to use in attacking me. Their reality was a household where their mother had no agency and where their father ensured that their mother was diminished over and over again. They witnessed my walking around on eggshells to maintain as much peace in the home as possible, and they learned to do the same. Gerry is a natural at gaslighting, manipulation, and intimidation, which were daily events in our house. The verbal onslaughts as part of this psychological warfare were the most dehumanizing and became worse with time. It was almost like a game: How much could one human take?

By the time the two oldest were school age, not a day went by that I wasn't called lazy, pathetic, crazy, insane, psycho, or useless. I was mocked for my appearance, eating habits, and of course for my parenting. The more miserable Gerry was toward me, the harder I worked to be a better spouse and mom. I was convinced I was the problem because there was no way someone who loved me would say these things if it wasn't true. I was trauma bonded—staying through the bad waiting on one little crumb of "good" to hold on to. It's like Gorilla Glue.

When Gerry didn't get his way, there was always hell to pay. He would throw the TV remote, cell phone, punch walls/doors, shake his fist at me or hit the counter, and abuse our family dog. This should have been a sign to me—but again, it was easier to pretend it wasn't so bad than to enrage him further. Gerry seemed to enjoy using the car as a weapon, driving erratically and scaring me and then speeding up when

I begged him to slow down. He would often threaten to kick me out of the car when he was enraged or I had asked the "wrong" question. Sometimes he would drive after drinking, and if I objected, he would shame me into submission.

Gerry traveled for work for extended periods of time and was often unavailable when away on these business trips. I was gaslit into believing that I was controlling by asking where his business was going to be and why he didn't call and check in with me or the children or respond to my phone calls. It became clear that when he was away, I was not to "bother" him and that just like when he was home, the responsibilities of parenting were mine to carry alone.

One time, he came home from a business trip with a hickey on his neck. When I asked who gave it to him, he told me I did. I had never given him a hickey, not even when we were teenagers, but his tactic worked. I was gaslit and questioned why I didn't remember giving him a hickey. I stopped inquiring of his whereabouts or who he was with. It was easier to ignore his lack of accountability than to try to express a concern or a worry. I constantly questioned myself and wondered, *Am I crazy? Am I losing my mind?* or *Maybe I AM the problem.* I later learned that he had been unfaithful for much of the marriage.

Gerry's level of emotional support for me personally was abysmal. He actually seemed annoyed anytime I was unwell, became distant and withheld affection, often insisting the pain was not that bad or all in my head. Experts call this stonewalling. When

I was in labor with our second child, he told me that I was imagining things. I went out for a walk alone and ended up coming back to the house begging him to take me to the hospital. I delivered our daughter two hours later. I contracted the swine flu/N1H1 while he was away for work during my pregnancy with our youngest child. He wouldn't come home to help me. I now realize he never had any regard for me and has little ability to empathize.

My ex treats our children's illnesses or concerns similarly, even when affirmed by physicians. He has denied treatment, including attempting to prevent me from getting one of our children to the hospital for alcohol poisoning. Most recently, two of our children have exhibited disordered eating behaviors. One had the physical symptoms of her disordered eating visible on her skin, including lanugo, the appearance of fine soft hair on her body, as well as extreme weight loss. He told our daughter on numerous occasions that she needed to lose weight so she could increase her speed for her sport. This sport is everything to her—and it is because of her father that this sport became everything to her. So, of course she wanted to get faster. I have to believe he knows the repercussions of his words. It's not just me that has expressed concerns but numerous professionals, family, and friends. He totally ignored our pleas, and when asked under oath during our custody proceedings, he claimed that she was perfectly healthy and in the best shape of her life.

Our youngest is now expressing his own obsession with weight. This is their father. He talks about weight and appearances often and criticizes eating habits, as he did with me for years. I have been told by experts that eating disorders may be a manifestation of the trauma that occurs when living in a coercively controlling environment. I don't doubt this. When a child feels so out of control in other parts of their life and food intake becomes the focus, it makes sense that they may attempt to gain control of their life by controlling food intake.

I finally filed for divorce in 2019, which resulted in a five-year legal battle. I was diagnosed with a precancerous condition shortly after I filed. This was during the pandemic and Gerry was refusing to have the children adhere to COVID protocols, which could have compromised my treatment. After numerous communications begging him to cooperate, I felt I had no choice but to have my attorney send a letter addressing these concerns. When Gerry received the letter, he called me screaming, "You fucking whore—I'm going to destroy you." He made it clear that I had embarrassed him by sending the letter, making him look like a terrible father. He also told me, "When I am done with you, my parents and the kids won't want anything to do with you."

Perhaps it was the scare of cancer and his reaction to the attorney's letter that created the clarity I needed. The memories flooded back and I realized Gerry is not a good father or person. He was becoming more physically violent with the children. He had held our daughter against the wall by her throat, thrown my oldest son around in physical altercations, pulled my youngest son's hair and often grabbed him, leaving marks on his arms, neck, back, and stomach—all in attempts to control them. All of my fawning from childhood began to dissipate.

Since the separation, Gerry's abusive behaviors toward me intensified—his promise to me made real— that he would "destroy me" and ensure the children "know you for who you really are." I'm certain that the children continue to hear the name-calling and false narratives about me when they are with him. He coerces them with material items, and I now understand that their aligning with him is simply easier than going against him. They are behaving like I did— anything to keep the risk of abandonment and rage at bay. Just like I had cognitive dissonance and didn't want to believe how horrible my ex was to me and our children, they also have cognitive dissonance.

As I write this, it is hard to believe that I am living in a world where our middle child, our daughter, is aligned with Gerry and repeating many of the phrases and words to me that she heard him say to me. Our youngest is struggling with how to not be rejected by his father yet knowing clearly that his father is unsafe.

It's different for our oldest. He has clarity because his father did physically abuse him, an incident none of us will ever forget. Gerry punched Mac in the face when he was sixteen years old. Mac called the police and left home for a few weeks. When Mac returned, he told me that he called the police for me so that I would see how terrible his dad was to me and so that I would leave. That was my wake-up call. My child needed to be hit in order for me to see that Gerry is an abuser.

Our daughter, battling an eating disorder, would soon be off to college. I realized that more parenting time with my youngest might be the best way to protect him and to prevent him from succumbing entirely to his father's controlling intimidation. He can see who his father is, and I had been educating him on the words to identify gaslighting and other harmful behaviors. But he, like his siblings, is forced to have a relationship with their father due to a family court system that does not acknowledge coercive control as an abuse of the children. Ensuring that I could have more time and decision-making with my youngest was imperative to me. I didn't want him to suffer like his older siblings had suffered and continue to suffer.

I should have predicted the retaliation. Gerry, who had been using our daughter as a primary weapon, intensified his behaviors. He knew that this would be the thing that mattered the most to me. He lives five minutes away but my daughter was often refusing to come for her custodial time because he was sabotaging time with me by dangling carrots in front of her—her use of the car, her time with her siblings, and giving her the freedom and material items any teen would gladly accept—if she followed the rules he had in place. Those were: hate your mother, reject your mother, hate your siblings, and therefore hate yourself. That's the ultimate revenge, having a child act like a soldier in war against someone they are not supposed to hate. I can see how much pain she is in, but she is still living in the fog of the abuse, unable to see her father's behavior as abusive.

Perhaps the most significant betrayal in all of this was the stonewalling by my own attorney. There was a diminishing of my experiences even when I brought in the most well-regarded experts on the topic of coercive control. I was fighting for more parenting time with my youngest as well as the ability to make medical decisions. I had seen what happened with my daughter due to more time with my abusive ex. Her negative behaviors escalated with me.

My legal team didn't acknowledge his abusive behavior, my children were unable to see it clearly, and I was wondering what I had gotten myself into. No wonder victims stay. On top of this, as is typical in these types of cases, Gerry was using the legal system to financially abuse me and the system was aligning with him—post-separation abuse rearing its ugly head. This experience, the betrayal by the system, was as brutal as living with Gerry. And this is exactly what Gerry could have hoped for. He and his lawyer intentionally stalled the legal process until my older two children aged out so I would likely not be able to bring in his abuse of me and the children or police reports referencing this.

Throughout my legal battle—I call it a war—my lawyer told me that I had to play nice and not reference abuse. Additionally, my lawyer subsequently refused to read up on or take any training on coercive control unless I paid for it, even though the Canadian Divorce Act changed in 2021, referencing coercive and controlling behavior as family violence. I was advised that I should stop trying to prevent Gerry from spending time with my youngest and to simply end the proceedings.

My attorney, like most, was more worried about his reputation than the safety and welfare of my youngest child. I retained an expert from the United States, who recommended that I have full decision-making and sole parenting until my ex acknowledged the abuse and attended a treatment program. The expert included reference to famous studies, such as the Saunders study and Adverse Childhood Experiences study, highlighting flaws in the family law process. My lawyer, days after he filed my expert report, told me that he wouldn't be disappointed if the other side had the report "kicked out" because he was worried about losing his own credibility with the court. In a case management conference, shortly after my expert report was filed, it was apparent that the judge was irritated by my expert report, stating, "I don't understand this report. I have never seen one like this before, and have never heard of the Saunders study or ACEs." In this conference (via phone), I told my lawyer it was imperative that he reference the abuse. He literally stuttered the word *abuse* when he told the judge my concerns.

Even after this experience, I still naively believed that the legal process was fair and objective and there would be no way any reasonable judge could dispute my evidence at trial. However, leading up to a settlement conference, my legal team told me there was a risk that I could lose custody of my son if I insisted on raising the abuse, as it could come across as being obsessed and "alienating" my ex (the abuser!). I was unwilling to be silent and told my lawyer that it was a risk I would take. In the settlement conference with a different judge, my lawyer attempted to refer to the abuse, but she yelled at him, "Attorney X, you know better than to use that word in my courtroom without evidence," even though we had a copy of a CPS report substantiating physical and emotional abuse. When my lawyer drew her attention to the report, she said, "Grabbing a child and leaving marks hardly qualifies as abuse. It may be bad parenting at best, but it isn't abuse."

My lawyer then asked, "Would choking be considered abuse?" She rolled her eyes and said, "Well, I guess choking would be a little different." The judge was cold toward me and constantly interrupted when I was speaking. A couple weeks later, my lawyer told me that the judge was likely annoyed by my expert report and impatient with me because she had seen my financials and saw that I made as much income as her. I knew instantly I had to do whatever I could to get out of this legal situation and avoid trial, as there was a significant risk that the judge would be biased against me for no other reason than speaking my truth.

As I was actively trying to settle with my ex, a report on making parenting arrangements in cases with family violence was posted on the Department of Justice Canada website. I sent the details to my lawyer and told him that it was imperative that he refer to these recommendations in my offer to Gerry, and that the recommendations support my position and that of my expert. My lawyer avoided my emails and initially refused to read the report. He also told me there was no way Gerry would settle based on my offer. He again reminded me that he was the expert in the law and that I should listen to him. I told him that I understand he knows the law but that I am the expert on abuse, the needs of my children, and of course an expert on Gerry. Gerry would only settle if I stood up to him. I had acquiesced for years and all that did was make him push harder. I was going to push back now. He also told me, "You are crazy for offering to pay for all of the kids' expenses, including university." I had to explain to him on multiple occasions that by remaining in a shared expense arrangement, Gerry could retain control of me and thereby subsequently continue to control my daughter in college and my youngest.

I ended up having to go to my lawyer's office the day before a scheduled hearing to keep my expert report in at trial, refusing to leave until he sent my revised offer to my ex. He told me that I was risking Gerry not settling at all by sending an offer with my protective provisions in them (e.g., the ability to take my youngest to a doctor when he was sick, etc.). Two hours before the scheduled hearing the very next morning, I received a call telling me that Gerry wanted to settle and that they would use the hearing to have the order and the divorce finalized. My lawyer did not congratulate me or acknowledge that I was right. Instead, he sent an email to me fifteen minutes before I walked into court stating that my final bill was due immediately and he would not release any of my files including the final order or divorce documents until he was paid.

Although I now have a court order (issued late 2023), I realize that Gerry will continue to attempt to coercively control the kids and me. He has ramped up his covert tactics and has also threatened legal action on numerous occasions in the last few months to exert fear and panic. This won't stop until the family court system changes.

Since I have been exposed to this broken legal system, I have had other women (successful professionals) share their current/past experiences in the system with me—resulting in them developing mental health issues (e.g., PTSD, anxiety, depression, etc.), harm to their children, limited access to their children, material financial loss, impact on careers, etc. I have made a commitment to myself to find ways to advocate against family violence and promote change in the family legal system. Now that I know what I know, I can't stand back and pretend this injustice and human rights issue does not exist here in the very system that is presumably designed to protect. We need a global movement that is bigger than any movement in history.

NOTES

Faith's ex exerted his control over her for years. His blatant disregard for her and the children actually strengthened the trauma bond. She was tied to him, waiting patiently for the breadcrumbs he would give her—the intermittent reinforcement—the little pieces of good that she grasped in hopes that the relationship would improve so she could keep her family intact. As we have seen in other stories in this book, coercive controllers/narcissistic abusers know this is what matters most. The breadcrumbs—the few incidences of good—become a manipulation tactic to intensify the trauma bond. Faith held on tight for years and, as is typical, her abuser gave her fewer and fewer breadcrumbs. All the while, since day one, he was indoctrinating the children in a false narrative against her.

When Faith finally escaped the relationship, she put her faith in the justice system, that the years of abuse on her children would give her the right to care for her children, in particular her youngest. Instead, her attorney was hoping her expert witness testimony would get thrown out, and she was silenced for discussing the abuse that had occurred, even the abuse to her children.

Faith went so far as to share academic literature with her attorney, including recent research submitted to the Canadian Department of Justice explaining the need to intervene in family violence cases to recognize the harms experienced by children, whether the abuse is overt or covert (Jaffe et al. 2023). Additionally, in Canada the Divorce Act has recently been updated (in 2021), indicating that court decisions regarding children must be guided by only the best interests of the children. Yet all this information fell on deaf ears.

The one thing that Faith knows now is that her children suffered greatly from the very beginning. Katz (2016) and Callaghan and colleagues (2018) assert, as so many other researchers do, that children experience coercive control alongside their mothers. Faith knows that her children's healing is dependent upon her, as it is for all protective parents. She is working hard on repairing relationships wrought with trauma. This process is exhausting for protective parents who have suffered immensely and must parent children they could have never imagined would suffer unacknowledged child abuse. This requires a different type of parenting – therapeutic parenting – that not all protective parents are equipped to give. It's a marathon, not a sprint.

But always, protective parents are their children's saving grace. Perhaps Faith would have left sooner, as so many victims say they wish they had—but then what if it was the same result? What if no one acknowledged the abuse and she was caught in a struggle not just with one child, her youngest, but with all three? This is the plight of every protective parent: escaping or staying, there is no better answer.

—Dr. C

BRITNEY AND ME

Natasha's Story – United States

Thomas and I met in acting school in San Francisco right after the world managed to survive Y2K. I worked as a sales assistant in private wealth management at a well-known investing firm, comfortably steering myself through my late twenties. I had just moved from New York City where I had a full life of family and friends there. New York City was home to me.

Thomas was an engineer at a multinational digital communications technology corporation during the dot-com boom. He was not your ordinary awkward-introverted-off-the-charts-brilliant Silicon Valley nerd. Thomas was bubbling with charm and charisma. He spoke as if he was deeply passionate about the arts, his Caribbean heritage, and his European family. At least this is what he said, and his words were convincing when layered atop a French accent, enthusiastic cadence, and soul-penetrating stare. Looking back, I see now that he behaved more like a preacher or cult leader. I was too young and naive to notice or care.

Thomas was attending acting school in addition to his full-time work. He loved performing, and he hosted an in-house television show for his company. His makeup artist recognized his talent and referred him to the same acting school I attended. Each week, Thomas appeared in full makeup fresh off-set. He was often late, entering at the same time as me, carrying his laptop case. Since we were usually the last to arrive, we were paired for warm-up exercises. These seemed intimate in nature, at least compared to the sterile corporate environments we had just left from our workday. One involved studying each other's walk. I remember the time he asked me to raise my shirt in order for him to observe my gait more precisely. I complied. We were serious students, and nailing a character's physicality was critical. During other exercises, we were required to silently stare into each other's eyes while seated directly across from each other with knees touching.

Looking back, I can see how I was giddily attracted and extremely curious about this older, more worldly, and sophisticated dark-skinned man from the Caribbean with a French accent. From today's vantage, however, I can see how enrolling in acting school was the perfect way to hone his craft of hiding his harmful character traits. It has also only recently occurred to me how the acting exercises themselves fostered a false sense of trust and closeness. There was one warm-up activity where we were instructed to share childhood stories, plus significant victories and traumas straight from our own lives. I shared vulnerabilities. Little did I know, I was giving this man the ammunition he would later use against me.

Thomas was over a decade my senior and could cry on cue. He praised his mother for all her sacrifices that included her moving from the Caribbean island of Martinique to Europe in search of a better life. He described his mother as fiery, street-smart, and persevering. His father had left the island ahead of his wife and had the benefit of completing more education. Thomas emphasized that his father was not smarter than his mother, but only benefited from being a man and therefore allowed to stay in school. He always said, "We didn't have much money, but we had a lot of love." However, as more time went by and I watched their family dynamics, my intuition told me otherwise. But like so many victims and survivors, I suppressed my intuition.

Thomas and I began spending time with a group of theater friends from the Los Angeles area. We were not dating just yet, and I had an opportunity to move back east to New York City, to pursue my acting career. I left my position with the investing firm, and soon thereafter, we began our bicoastal dating relationship. After our first weekend together, Thomas invited me to tour Egypt with him. It was a once-in-a-lifetime trip. We became Egyptologists in our own right, visiting ancient sights, including the temples of Abu Simbel, as we cruised up the Nile on *The Oberoi Zahra*. We raced camels across Giza, took a private tour of the pyramids, and I photographed Thomas lying inside a sarcophagus as if he was the Pharaoh positioned in his final resting place.

In the fall of 2001, after a year of dating, Thomas invited me to Martinique to meet his mother's family. When they were young, his father and mother could not afford to travel with all the children. Thomas was the only person in his family who had never been back to the island. What I did not see coming was the staging for his marriage proposal. We had talked about it and even had some test runs where he would pop the question just to ensure my positive response. Thomas is not one to risk failure. When we arrived, marriage was the last thing on my mind, as the focus was on meeting his mother's family and traversing the island.

As always, Thomas managed to keep my rational mind guessing, which was an adrenaline rush during dating but a destabilizing influence during later attempts at creating an ordinary family life. We arrived at a resort and received our welcome drinks before being escorted to the penthouse suite, which he had filled with vases of tropical white flowers. Next, Thomas insisted that we lie together on the bed where he read the poem he had penned on Egyptian papyrus, a keepsake from our trip. It ended with him asking me to marry him. Of course I said, "Yes," just as we'd rehearsed. The next day, we met his relatives who immediately referred to me as "the little wife." I looked like a ghost in photographs because of my Anglo-European skin compared to their much darker Afro-Caribbean complexions.

We headed back to New York in time for Thomas's fortieth birthday celebration. On the plane, I noticed him writing the guest list for our wedding. I told him I would prefer to elope. He said, "No. I'm the only boy. My mum has to be there." The idea of a large wedding also made my family very happy and endeared him into their hearts even more. Thomas frequently spoke of the global lifestyle we would lead. In addition to flying back and forth between New York City and Silicon Valley, we regularly took trips to see his family in Europe, tacking on trips to London, Paris, Dublin, Edinburgh, or elsewhere.

I thought we were on the same wavelength when I accepted his proposal. However, what I see now is that my acceptance of the proposal was the tightening of his grip. After our engagement, I was the one who moved into his world—leaving my urban existence behind, my home base in New York City, and my apartment in Santa Monica. Thomas's sprawling ranch was located in the California desert. I would soon realize I was isolated and alone. It felt like I was living in a foreign country.

The day after moving in together, we took a vacation, where he slept for an entire week. I had never seen him so exhausted. When I expressed concern, he lectured me about hard work and the real world. He treated me like a spoiled child who needed to learn that playtime had ended. Soon thereafter, I was instructed to start looking for work. Again, we lived out of the city in a remote desert town. I had never navigated the freeways and didn't feel confident doing so now, let alone the various corridors of his compound. I was chastised for moving an antique chair, and when I suggested that we redecorate the master suite before the wedding, he said I needed to get a job to pay for it myself. One afternoon while reading on the sofa, I noticed a camera pointing directly at me. After I unplugged it, Thomas called to ask what was wrong and made a joke, gaslighting me about the camera. Already having a loss of autonomy, I didn't press the issue.

Thomas's stalking and isolation tactics tore apart my existence and ambitions as if they were the silly dreams of a girl. He would tell me that my friends and even my family complained about my having "silly dreams." I believed him when he told me this and couldn't wrap my head and my heart around who I was becoming. I later would see it as the bait and switch typical of these abusers: The Thomas I was partnered with was not the Thomas advertised to me. I felt myself slipping away, lost on the downward spiral, my brain not functioning properly. I threw myself into yoga in a community an hour away. Yoga was the only thing that seemed to help me remain steady. After six months, I gained much clarity. Within the toxicity of the home environment, filled with consistent arguments, feelings of overwhelm, constantly being picked apart, and my finances depleting, I recognized I had to leave.

While I was packing boxes, Thomas pulled me away and held me tight against his chest. He said, "It took me this long to find you. I'm not going to let you leave this way." He said I could stay at home and write, then promised we would find a home in the community I loved when we were ready to start a family. I fell back into line. But of course, this was an empty promise he never planned to keep. It was designed to capture me and keep me in his grips.

I was ecstatic when I found out I was pregnant and loved being a mother to our son, Josh. I spent the summer of 2007 caring for our newborn and asking Thomas for that family home he had promised. I was tired of being isolated. Thomas had amnesia, however. Eventually, when Josh was ready for preschool, Thomas allowed me to enroll him in this community an hour away from the ranch. I had connections there with yoga friends who helped me create a home base. Thomas would stay with us one night each week, and Josh and I were expected to return to the ranch every weekend. I'm not sure why Thomas allowed this, but I assume it was because the idea of the family home gave the appearance of him being a "good" father, yet he was still able to have little obligations to our son and retained his freedom. This time away from Thomas and the ranch became a safe haven for me. This went on for several years.

When Thomas's father passed away, it seemed like a breaking point for him. He broke up with me by text. I was given salary requirements. Next, we started a string of therapy appointments that I had hoped would lead to positive co-parenting. I had been going on my own for years —trying to make sense of it all and wondering what was wrong with me. At one point, Thomas and I actually made amends and tried again to make the relationship work. But that was short-lived. Therapy after that, when I had disengaged and wasn't willing to "try again," resulted in me being constantly diagnosed and mental health shamed. Thomas insisted that my own therapist told him I was a borderline and to end it with me immediately. I was so confused. Could this be true?

Eventually, I would realize that there is a dark side to an industry that preys upon marital misfortunes and the vulnerabilities of women and targets the children specifically. Children are the collateral damage once you start your case. Even with the phrase "in the best interest of the children" being tossed around, the opposite occurs with greater frequency. I now refer to this racket as designer human trafficking. And I was Thomas's *plaything*—a term a court professional once used in describing me.

What happened next was something I never could have foreseen: My child was one of these humans trafficked, while custody evaluations and "therapeutic" professionals diminished me as the protective parent. I recently learned that my child has been pried out of my arms by the same professionals who crafted the conservatorship for Britney Spears. I have always felt a close kinship with Britney and deeply empathized with her struggles. Now I understand that it was not too much of a stretch. The same bullying tactics and legal strategy were used by some of the same professionals to take away our children, put us to work, break us down, medicate us, hold us accountable through a therapeutic team, make sure that we are earning, and enforce salary requirements.

Currently, my son only spends time with me when he is at the dentist. His father provides transportation to and from the appointments because my sweet boy now states—after years of indoctrination—that he does not feel safe being in the car with me. Josh has false memories and—as with so many children who are coercively controlled—he has been gaslit and pulled away from the loving arms of his protective parent. His anxiety is untreated because the systems do not recognize that he is trapped in the covert web of his father, the coercive controller/narcissistic abuser.

During the last meeting with the parenting coordinator, who I believe to be corrupt along with so many other players in my case, my ex's lawyer argued that Josh should live full time with the abuser since he is sixteen years of age and doing well in school, and that he should be focused on getting into a top university. Unfortunately, the parenting coordinator, supposedly a neutral third party, plays into the mental-health-shaming narrative created by my ex and his legal team and will not make any decisions that support my relationship with my child. For example, the terms of our custody agreement stipulate that Thomas and I plan Josh's summer schedule and share weekly updates with one another. My ex does neither, yet this is ignored by the parenting coordinator. Instead of looking out for the best interests of our child and working on repairing the harm my ex has inflicted by intentionally blocking contact between Josh and me, the parenting coordinator mandates therapy for me and now another full custody evaluation. If Thomas isn't cooperating with the current custody plan and the parenting coordinator is not ensuring he does, then how will a custody evaluation help the relationship between me and Josh? This is Thomas's plan—to fracture the attachment between us—and the parenting coordinator is witnessing it before her eyes yet doing nothing.

Josh's therapist also does not recognize the importance of my role in my child's life. In fact, this therapist seems to have replaced me as the co-parent. When I have tried to remove this individual as a therapist because of the evident undermining of my relationship with my son, my ex has been emboldened. He has submitted to the court that my son prefers the therapist in his life over me. The therapist is yet another person used to reinforce my ex's agenda, and he is compensated well for this.

At least now I have new words I did not possess during the relationship with Thomas. They are: *gaslight, narcissistic abuse, coercive control, vexatious litigation, DARVO (deny, attack, reverse victim and offender), post-separation abuse,* and *betrayal blindness.* I think I learned them in that order.

NOTES

The coercive controller/narcissistic abuser was an aspiring actor and ended up pulling off the greatest role of all time. He was able to make Natasha believe in him and their love. She found out too late that his whole life was a facade and that she unknowingly became his "toy," an object. Had she seen that his tactics were to charm her and saw through the façade, she may have been able to escape before the abuse escalated and before he was able to weaponize their son and take him away from her.

Coercive controllers/narcissistic abusers attempt to maliciously fracture the child's attachment to their protective parent. Thomas has excelled at this and young Josh is caught in a state of confusion and trauma bonded. Children will often align with the more powerful parent simply because that feels safer. They know all too well that aligning with the protective parent may in fact mean that the child receives the same treatment as that (targeted) parent. No child wants to take that risk. Hart and colleagues (2002), Brassard and Donovan, (2006) and Stark and Hester (2019) describe trauma bonding in such situations as a deliberate brainwashing, during which the individual who is the coercive controller purposefully weakens the child's autonomy, much as they have the autonomy of the parent who has been targeted, through the manipulation tactics of coercive control.

Natasha is still fighting to show her son who she really is—and to diminish the false narrative that he has now heard for years living under the regime of the coercive controller/narcissistic abuser. Thankfully, she realizes that she has so much influence even in short visits and few interactions with her child. Josh will gain clarity with her continuing to show up and reminding him of his attachment to her and her unconditional love.

The trauma for protective mothers is persistent —the abuse never ends. The narrative that coercive control, when acknowledged, is exclusively inter-parental, is false. As

Andreea Gruev-Vintali states (2023) in her seminal book, Coercive Control: At the Heart of Domestic Violence, *"coercive control through legal harassment before the family court judge and the children's judge is one of the most effective legal-looking means used by controlling and coercive men to further crush the rights of women and children while continuing to attack the women's financial resources" (122). It's what happened to Britney Spears. It's what is happening to Natasha and her son and to so many protective mothers worldwide.*

— Dr. C

MUNCHAUSEN BY PROXY

Ana's Story – United States

When I met my ex-husband, Scott, I was drawn to his deep love for his family, which brought us closer as we got to know each other and our families. I fell in love with a man who I thought was generous, kind, and funny. Although I noticed his frequent short temper, Scott often blamed it on his stressful job. I never considered it might be part of a larger problem.

Scott would get angry if I forgot to leave the outdoor lights on for him. He'd say I was incapable of respecting my husband, calling me the C-word, bitch, and other things to verbally assault me. He'd get mad if he came home and I was working on a project—he'd yell, "Why would you pick NOW to do this project when I'm just getting home? I thought you'd have dinner on the table." He called me incessantly when our children were newborns to make sure they were on a strict feeding schedule. It was the eat, sleep, play method. If they were sleeping when he called, he would make me wake them up. This during their infancy. If they were falling asleep, he made me shake rattles in their face so they would stay awake until it was time to sleep. I could never get anything right—I was walking on eggshells all the time. I knew that I had better respond as he demanded.

I look back now and I realize that there were red flags all along the way. When I was in labor for my oldest, I needed an emergency C-section. Scott became enraged. Through clenched teeth, he told me that if his mother could deliver five children naturally, then I should be able to do the same. As I was wheeled away for surgery in tears, he looked at me with disgust. He left the hospital and returned once very briefly. A nurse asked me if everything was okay. I told her that Scott had lots of work demands. She knew what I couldn't say out loud: that Scott had no regard for me.

Scott later told me I would be rewarded if I delivered our next child vaginally. Sophie was born vaginally. Like with Quinn, Scott came to the hospital for delivery and then left to go to work. When I called him at his office that day, Scott screamed at me for bothering him.

This marked for me the beginning of a pattern of cruel and controlling behavior that subjected my children and me to confusing torment that continues now even after our divorce. It's obvious Scott was always wanting to exert power over me, but when he began to be a tyrant around Quinn and Sophie, I couldn't ignore it.

It took about ten years, but I finally got up the courage and filed for divorce. I had been the primary caretaker and foolishly asked Scott to move out. He wouldn't leave. I decided to stay in the home until the details of who would live where were decided, not realizing Scott's abusive behavior would get worse. And it did. Scott took my staying in the home to mean that he could control my space everywhere. He would intimidate me, coming into the bedroom where I slept and standing over me, going into fits of rage and following me around the house screaming and yelling and verbally assaulting me. I never knew what would set him off. I asked my attorney if I could file a restraining order—forcing Scott out of the home—and he advised me that it wouldn't look good to do so because I hadn't left the home. Eventually, I had no choice and moved out.

Before our separation, Sophie became very sick, and we sought help from two physicians at Stanford Hospital. Sophie was diagnosed with a chronic inflammatory disorder, and after several months of treatment, she made a full recovery. Scott supported Sophie's diagnosis and treatment, often commenting on her progress. Despite warnings by the doctors that the condition might return, I felt secure knowing Sophie was in the care of esteemed professionals. She remained under the care of these Stanford doctors through the finalization of our divorce.

And then just like that, Sophie's medical team was dismantled. A week after the divorce, a new narrative emerged: that I was unstable and was faking my daughter's illness. Scott disputed Sophie's diagnosis and blocked our access to her team. I assumed that with documented evidence by two specialists at Stanford that nothing would change. I had no idea the lengths Scott was willing to go.

Scott sent multiple emails accusing me of Munchausen syndrome by proxy (MSP), now known as medical child abuse (MCA) or factitious disorder imposed on another (FDIA). It is when a caregiver makes up or causes health problems in someone under their care. I was shocked. I couldn't believe that Scott would make such an accusation. I was also confused. He had been supporting Sophie's healing process all along—until we divorced. What changed? We had the nation's leading experts engaged in Sophie's treatment, and the treatment worked! Scott went so far as to claim the doctors had medicated Sophie with toxic treatments.

Reeling from this, I couldn't imagine any of Scott's allegations would hold water. Yet, within a few months, a family court-appointed professional—a parenting coordinator—ruled in his favor. For all intents and purposes, I was deemed "unstable." Sophie was no longer able to see her team of doctors nor receive the treatment that alleviated her symptoms. Scott now claims that he "does not recall our daughter ever being diagnosed and treated by two Stanford physicians." Worse, when I make suggestions or ask for more information from doctors or anyone on Sophie's new team, Scott describes feelings of being "unsafe" with me, claiming I am trying to sabotage Sophie's treatment for her *replacement* diagnosis of acute anxiety disorder. He tells team members—who are on his team—that I am creating an "air of hostility." This is a DARVO tactic—where coercive controller/narcissistic abusers deny wrongdoing, attack the actual victim, and reverse victim and offender. He is accusing me of exactly what he is doing.

Perhaps most shocking to me was that Sophie's original team of physicians didn't feel the need to report Scott's allegations and unwillingness to continue a treatment that was evidently working for Sophie. They all became complicit, simply by doing nothing. I was in a state of shock. Was I crazy? What had just happened? How could the best doctors refuse to give treatment to our daughter? How did Scott coerce them into silence—and convince the parent coordinator appointed by family court that Sophie didn't need treatment? I now know I have been experiencing medical gaslighting. The parent coordinator listened to a father's allegations rather than reading documentation by nationally known physicians about my child's welfare. And the judge didn't question this.

As expected, without treatment, Sophie relapsed a year later. A new medical team, chosen by my ex, was appointed. He has undermined any efforts for Sophie to receive the treatment she had previously. He tells the medical team that I have Munchausen syndrome by proxy and that my "paranoia" is making Sophie sick. He continues to make false statements about my poor parenting. I wrongly assumed that any new doctors would conduct a full evaluation and consult with Sophie's previous physicians before making a determination. Isn't that protocol? This has not occurred.

In the meantime, Sophie continues to be compromised, suffering debilitating symptoms that prevent her from attending school and doing her favorite things, like dance. She is sad and confused. Her dad disallows her from speaking of her illness and she is forbidden from ever mentioning the previous diagnosis to "his" ' medical team. Scott tells Sophie I made it all up. I have been virtually silenced. If I speak up, I worry that I may be stripped of any parenting time due to my "instability."

When Sophie is with her father, he makes her run sprints while recording and ridiculing her, all in an attempt to prove she is not ill. Again, he insists that her illness is "all in her head" and tells her so. Despite having 50-50 legal custody, Scott threatens legal action if I suggest taking Sophie for an appointment to follow up on her care. He and his chosen doctors also send emails instructing me to tell Sophie that nothing is wrong.

Sophie's older brother, Quinn, is Scott's "favorite" child. Quinn is healthy and an athlete. Sophie often tells me how she wishes that she could be more like Quinn and wishes her dad loves her as much as Quinn. For his part, Quinn has figured out how not to get into trouble with Scott but also tries to be a buffer between Scott and Sophie. I know he is working hard to distract his dad's focus on proving Sophie is not suffering from a disorder. Both of my children are suffering.

As a mother, being scrutinized by my children's doctors due to my ex-husband's false allegations of medical child abuse is both heartbreaking and traumatizing. We lost Sophie's team of experts and are now forced to see physicians chosen by Scott. Every appointment feels like an interrogation. The probing eyes and the questioning of my every word and action often means I am in an emotionally distressed state. The situation is compounded by the undue admiration all of these individuals seem to have for Scott, who, armed with his Ivy League education, casts a long shadow over my credibility. It feels like an uphill battle where Scott's academic prestige trumps my lived experience and genuine care for my children, leaving me feeling isolated and unjustly vilified in my role as a mother.

For over fifteen years during our marriage, no physician ever questioned my credibility or worried about my actions in seeking guidance during my children's medical routine appointments, until now. Although I believe the doctors now see through him, they remain reluctant to help because of his status. I'm sure they fear legal repercussions. Scott is intimidating and is clear that his narrative is the one the team should be listening to: His daughter is not ill. This has created a vicious cycle where Sophie's health continues to deteriorate.

Throughout it all, I have tried to advocate for our Sophie while privately sinking under the weight of verbal attacks and the fear of the damage her father continues to inflict. There is an assumption of two high-conflict individuals in a divorce, but in reality, one is the coercive controller/narcissistic abuser and the other is the protector. Scott continues to use fear and intimidation to make me comply and opposes anything I suggest, so I have tried to speak to physicians and teachers in private. For example, when a teacher proposed offering classes via Zoom for Sophie during her absence, I mistakenly expressed approval. Sophie's father immediately opposed the extra support while angrily accusing me of making too many accommodations for her.

As a mother, I've been navigating a painful journey, watching my children's childhoods slip away due to circumstances beyond our control. The denial of critical medical treatments by my ex, coupled with false allegations of Munchausen by proxy and child abuse, has shattered our world. False accusations and medical manipulation by my ex have turned our lives upside down. Scott's relentless attempts to control every aspect of our children's lives extend beyond medical care. He uses my daughter's support team to send daily emails questioning my mental stability and parenting abilities, forcing me to defend myself against multiple, baseless accusations. Every visit to my daughter's school, every glance at her drifting from friends, and every dance team victory stings with the reminder of what should have been.

His goal is clear: to break me down mentally, emotionally, and financially. And both Quinn and Sophie suffer because of this.

The emotional toll on our daughter is profound. She feels trapped between conflicting narratives, struggling to understand why her father dismisses her pain and suffering. Her once bright and hopeful demeanor has dimmed, replaced by anxiety and confusion. Sophie fears expressing her symptoms, knowing her father's reaction will be harsh and dismissive. She shares with me how she recalls feeling better after her treatment but that she knows she cannot say this out loud. This internal conflict has affected her academic performance and social interactions, isolating her further from her peers.

My efforts to seek help and advocate for Sophie's well-being are often met with skepticism. Society's tendency to assume mutual fault in divorces that involve high-conflict spouses makes it difficult for the truth to emerge. The isolation is suffocating, but I refuse to give up.

In the meantime, through tears, Sophie begs me to help make her well again.

NOTES

Ana's story is no different than others you have read in this book. A protective parent wanting nothing more than to ensure the physical and psychological well-being of her children. Yet Ana has been gaslit by her abuser and a court system that fails to acknowledge how her ex is undermining her child's care. More significantly, Ana has been gaslit by the medical establishment. Esteemed physicians have chosen to ignore her child's illness, all to keep an abuser complacent. We rely on the medical establishment to follow their ethical guidelines and what many refer to as the Hippocratic oath: "primum non nocere," to "first, do no harm."

Beyond that, this medical establishment is complicit in the pathologizing of a mother who is attempting to protect her child. It typifies the reality of coercive control. If someone has the character traits of a coercive controller/narcissistic abuser, then they will exert power over others and collaborate with the systems, in this case both family court and the medical system, to inflict institutional betrayal.

Diagnoses are supposed to be made by experts in the field, yet Ana has been diagnosed by her ex-husband and a parenting coordinator! Munchausen syndrome by proxy is identified in the Diagnostic and Statistical Manual of Mental Disorders (DSM-5)—*the "bible" for mental health professionals and researchers diagnosing and classifying mental disorders—as a syndrome that most frequently occurs in women. It is often referred to as factitious disorder imposed on another (FDIA) and is known as a form of medical child abuse (DSM-5 2013). We live in a world where women are pathologized for wanting to protect their children and Munchausen syndrome by proxy is co-opted frequently by abusive parents in order to pathologize a healthy protective parent. As Dr. Evan Stark highlighted, women attempting to protect their children are often given "pseudo-psychiatric" labels deflecting the attention away from abusers and their behaviors (Stark, 2012). Patriarchal ideology permeates institutions and victims often experience gaslighting by the very systems intended to protect them.*

The trope of the "crazy woman" is reinforced within patriarchal norms, with the stereotyping and labeling of women's behaviors often based upon misogynistic ideology. This "crazy" and "mentally unstable" labeling cre-

ates further oppression. When the labels are applied in an already oppressive system, such as family court and our medical establishment, it becomes evident that women are swimming up against a strong current. Research completed in Canada by Susan Zaccour (2018) affirms that "ableist labels are used especially by fathers, but also by judges and experts, to diminish mothers' credibility and attack their parental capacity" (58). Mothers become trapped by a system that is supposed to protect our most vulnerable, in this case, protect and treat Sophie. Ana is walking a tightrope. Fight for Sophie to be treated or run the risk of losing custody of Sophie and perhaps Quinn too.

— Dr. C

IVY LEAGUE SCANDAL

Lily's Story – United States

_____

We were picture-perfect—a wealthy family with three adopted boys living on the tranquil edge of one of the country's most beautiful lakes. Our boys had everything; they were exceptional alpine ski racers and bright students. Their father was a successful start-up millionaire from Silicon Valley. I was a devoted, loving stay-at-home mom with a pristinely polished house and handsomely groomed kids. From outside appearances, we were flawless. But for decades, behind closed doors, I had endured the abuse at the hands of my coercive controller. We met when I was just fifteen; he was nineteen. He quickly had me flying high with the notion that he was the perfect man, slowly and methodically shaping me into the perfect victim.

I was physically abused early in our relationship, but most of his tactics were psychological in nature: gaslighting, manipulation, intimidation, and isolation. As a teenager, I was isolated from friends when he questioned their worthiness. It became easier to abandon these relationships rather than risk his wrath if I disobeyed. I was told to lie to his family and friends about my age, telling them that I was a student at an elite university, all the while still attending high school. I was ashamed. I avoided others to protect myself from the weight of the shame. As a result, I could not be myself and the relationships I forged were shallow. No one really knew me. I did not know me.

The coercive control intensified as time went by, but I did not know any better and certainly did not see that I was in an abusive relationship. My ex, Marc, would force me to comply with his demands and when I disagreed, the results were always the same: threats of abandonment on the roadside if in the car or suffering during weeks of the silent treatment (stonewalling). Those silent periods were so destabilizing that I begged for his forgiveness when I had done nothing wrong. His moments of rage seemed unpredictable, but now I know they were a way to modify my behavior and force me into compliance.

Every girl witnesses society's betrayal of victims, and that left me discouraged that anyone, even my parents, would believe my stories of abuse. Never mind the fact that the abuse was so nuanced and confusing that I could not fully comprehend the gravity of its nature. As the years passed, the financial tether to Marc became insurmountable, and he amassed a greater fortune than I had ever dreamed possible. I endured this abuse for thirty years, and despite the times I tried to leave, I was always presented with a reason to stay.

But things changed in 2012. We fled the Bay Area after the epic failure of Marc's high-profile start-up. We moved to a sleepy little town on the edge of this beautiful lake, hoping to leave behind the chaos of Silicon Valley for a more peaceful life. But chaos and abuse remained. The location had changed, but my bigger-than-life spouse had not. He was hyper-focused on the two older sons' education and ski racing. He funded the construction of a K-8 charter school in this area where our boys attended. But his charity disguised his true deceptive nature, and this "good deed" was only a part of his ploy to have our small community worship him.

In 2019, clarity seeped in. I asked for a divorce. Knowing Marc would retaliate, I was more fearful than ever, but I was exhausted and knew deep to my core that the relationship was abusive. I had to leave. Now I know why so many prefer the term *escape*. While I had contemplated leaving for years, I was unprepared for the post-separation abuse. The divorce proceedings forced disclosure of our financials of which I had little to no access to throughout our marriage. In the end, after years of family court proceedings, I found out that Marc had mismanaged our family assets to nearly zero. He presented a false narrative to everyone else, leading people to believe he had multiple millions. Me, with no agency after years of this abuse, didn't have the voice to tell anyone otherwise.

I was forced to leave and experienced a life I had never imagined. I literally went from riches to rags. I lived with a friend, worked part time as a baker, all the while trying to maintain a shred of time with my sons, but instead I was embroiled in what I now know to be the playbook for abusers. Marc used the children and the legal system to punish me. The children, as with so many, became his choice weapon against me.

My intent was to build a new life as a single mother of three. However, Marc took every opportunity to sabotage my loving relationship with our boys. His gaslighting techniques were used far and wide as a shield to prevent others from knowing his true self and his flailing financial crisis, now being exerted onto my boys. The wedge between this mother and her children grew. Their father reinforced the lies, using the financial resources intended to be my half of any settlement to pay for, and used various "interventions"— therapists, attorneys, mediators, custody evaluators, judges, guardian ad litem, the police, and even my children's teachers—to enforce his false narrative. He relied on the fact that the family courts were slow and ineffective. Marc used their mere presence in the process to give weight to his false allegations. He ran circles around these professionals, and many of them muddled the issues when they spoke with our boys. As a result, my loving relationship with my boys was being destroyed before my eyes.

While my team of attorneys had successfully finalized our divorce, there were still issues of custody to resolve. In the meantime, I shifted my focus to our boys' education. Marc had strictly controlled their education, even going so far as to write their papers and take their at-home tests. I was forbidden to have any input, as the legal fees were mounting. I became worried when our sixteen-year-old son decided to graduate high school a year early and began applying to universities, completing forty-six-plus applications. I wanted to participate in the application process, but neither my ex nor my son would allow me. Marc's penchant for lying and exaggerating reality made me concerned that something foul was afoot. I contacted my son's local school and asked questions about his grades. I discovered Marc was manipulating the grades between his online classes and local high school. Neither school knew that all nine Bs were changed to As and then transferred to my son's final transcript from his graduating school. Our son did not have a 4.0 GPA, but no one was the wiser.

I brought this to the attention of my attorney because I feared Marc was committing college application fraud. I had become aware that our son was already receiving acceptance letters and scholarships to various schools. I knew our son was potentially committing state and federal crimes, and I would be complicit if I didn't act.

My attorney made a bold move, and we filed an emergency motion with the family court without notice to Marc, requesting the court to order my ex to share all the college application information and halt any acceptances. The court granted our request, and we served Marc, but he ignored the court's ruling and proceeded with the college admission process. The court had to order him three times to halt the process and provide all applications and data, but he refused.

It would appear that my ex was not bound to comply with any court order or law.

As a result of the court order, our son's local high school shared a copy of an Ivy League university application, and before me laid more lies and exaggerations—essays written by someone other than my son, and achievements and awards never gained or given. The falsified information went so far as to claim that my son had received two United States patents while working collaboratively with a founding software engineer at his father's start-up. The list goes on and on: the development of an app, a prominent job under my ex's tutelage beginning at the age of thirteen, and lineage as a Native American. The entire application was a web of lies and a manufactured reality of my son's academic achievements, barely clinging to some truths about my son.

Marc had been cunning and used loopholes in the application process to gain acceptance into fifteen schools, with more to come and over $800,000 in academic scholarships awarded. During a global pandemic, my ex had seized upon a moment in history to optimize our son's chances of getting into some top-tier universities since schools did not require standardized test results (SAT or ACT). Marc operated like a wolf in sheep's clothing, using his charm and ability to con and manipulate a system that wasn't even looking for this type of outright fabrication.

Remember, I was navigating this from afar. I was doing what I did in the relationship: attempting to fix a situation that I thought perhaps would end with greater clarity for the system that had worked against me and perhaps give my children clarity. I wanted our son to withdraw his applications and reapply with accurate information. We asked forty-six universities for copies of applications submitted, but privacy laws (FERPA, the Family Educational Rights and Privacy Act) shielded my son's secrets. I contacted the various people and organizations my son claimed to have worked with, but they did the same and either ignored or told me to ask my son for the information. Marc hired a top criminal attorney who advised him and our son to plead the Fifth. At this point, I realized committing the crime was easier than unraveling it. Time was running out; if my son accepted an offer, he would get caught and pay a price for his father's sins. At the very least, our son would have to start his adult life based on lies, a similar burden I had to live with due to decades under the control of a master manipulator and pathological liar.

As I'm sure most can imagine, these attempts by me to right a wrong, to give clarity to the harmful systems that betrayed me and my children, and more importantly to show my children who their father really is, only incited my abuser more. All the while I was seeing my sons at his discretion, and as we know with many of these abusers, the smear campaign intensified. I defended myself against false claims of child abuse, used mediators to draft a fair parenting agreement my ex loosely followed, and relied on the courts to reign him in. He had instructed our older boys to record our private conversations during my parenting time and then used those illegal recordings to undermine my parental authority and shame me.

Eventually, Marc's use of these systems and the manipulation of my children and the chaos he had created in my home with our boys became overwhelming. He drained my savings and pushed me into a deep depression. As a result, I became destabilized and confrontational. I installed security cameras due to his abuse claims to protect myself from further allegations. One of my sons became physically abusive, and I feared for my safety. Visits by the local police (at my ex's request) were becoming commonplace during my custody time. I felt my boys slipping away, and at the same time, I was detaching from them. My once sweet and loving relationship with my sons was fractured because I had dared to leave an abusive marriage and exposed the college application fraud. I had to redefine what motherhood meant to me. I could no longer parent in the way I had envisioned long ago. My ex's need for control overshadowed my basic needs to grow and thrive, and I watched my ex begin to do the same to our boys. For our oldest, my sixteen-year-old, this meant denying him a chance to grow into an independent young adult.

As a result of Marc's college application fraud that implicated his current start-up in the crime, the company decided to buy out our founding shares, and we were once again flush with cash. We now had a significant war chest of funds. Millions of dollars were spent on each side; he used the court to shield the truth, and I used the courts to expose the abuse. One judge asked me: Will you be agreeable and surrender custody if I can get your legal fees paid? Some attorneys told me: Let the boy go to the elite school of his choice on application fraud and let him suffer the consequences. Our county judge told me to drop all forty-five contempt charges to streamline the case. In a moment of complete honesty from a child coercively controlled, my oldest told me he had no choice but to side with his father because he believed his father could get him further in life.

Fast forward a year later, and the college application case pales compared to the larger issue. Under the control of their father, my boys refused to see me. The courts became Marc's playground. He moved them to an undisclosed address and threatened legal action if I continued to ask him for their address. After three months of working through the court system, he was ordered to give their home address.

Marc filed for our oldest son to be emancipated by the court at age sixteen. His first attempt was denied, but a new judge granted our son's emancipation at age seventeen upon a second request. The judge refused to acknowledge the college application fraud, citing the matter was another court's jurisdiction. I had been gagged from presenting pertinent information regarding our son's entanglement with his father's illegal activities. As a result, our son was no longer seen as a minor in the eyes of the law. If he committed college application fraud, he would be held solely accountable under the law for his father's crimes. Their father had effectively used the emancipation of a minor to strip me of my parental rights. Emancipation was simply another strategy used to retaliate against me. My child continually living under the regime of the coercive controller, not free at all.

Four months passed, and Marc filed a termination of parental rights request for our middle son. This action is simply a de-mothering, the intent to erase me from all documents stating that I was his mother. Claims were made that I had abandoned our son. I had to meet with an investigator and present evidence showing I had made multiple attempts to be in his life. I brought pictures of all the cards, baked goods, and gifts I had sent him over the past year. I supplied evidence I had paid for his therapist and funded a college trust account. The investigator recommended my rights not be terminated. Marc was unsuccessful; however, the process traumatized me and likely our middle son, who had to write a letter saying why he didn't want me as his mother.

All this happened while we waited for a trial on the college application fraud and custody issues. I was waiting, but my abuser was busy finding ways to delay our trial. It had been delayed four times over two years at his request. I felt powerless to protect our boys and fell into an abyss of doom while my abuser kidnapped our boys in plain sight.

At the same time, Marc asked the court for a domestic violence restraining order against me. The court denied his initial request but pushed the issue to a hearing. Curiously, Marc found ways to repeatedly delay that hearing for various reasons. I was devastated that the court would even consider such a hearing, let alone agree to multiple postponements. At the time, I still saw our youngest son every other weekend. If his intent was genuine and he believed I was a threat to our boys, he would not have asked the court to postpone the restraining order hearing. But then it became clear why he would accuse me of domestic violence yet not follow through with the hearing. Its purpose was to intimidate me and validate to our boys that I was abusive on the fact alone that the court entertained such a request. In the eyes of our boys, I was proven guilty without a hearing. Again, Marc's false allegations and the court's platform had given weight to my ex's claims.

It also affected my parenting. I became fearful of spending time alone with our youngest son. I had already been falsely accused of molesting our middle son in court documents, so surely the same could be done with my youngest. I couldn't introduce our son to new people in my life for fear they'd be accused of horrible things. Marc had accused friends of abuse. I felt like I was in a tug-of-war with my ex; our boys were the rope. Erasing me from our children's lives is my punishment for daring to leave him and protect our boys. Despite having access to some of the best experts and attorneys, I felt my only option to end this painful and abusive tug-of-war was surrendering custody.

A divorce is final, but custody never is, and court litigation can continue until a child ages out of the system. The family court is supposed to protect vulnerable family members, but it functions very differently and facilitates the tug-of-war between parents, leaving one trapped with their abuser. After three and a half years, I stopped fighting for justice through the family court and devised creative solutions to keep contact with my boys that didn't rely on court orders. Every day is a balancing act: managing hope and fear for my children, trying to control my grief, and finding ways to protect my boys, knowing there is a system at odds with protecting the most vulnerable in our society. As a survivor who left the abuse, I hope to model a path forward for my boys' future escape. I pray that they see the truth one day.

NOTES

As Dr. Lisa Fontes states (2015) in her book Invisible Chains, *"women who get caught in the web of a controlling man are no different from other women. They just had the bad luck to become involved romantically with a controlling person at a time when they were especially vulnerable" (5). Lily was vulnerable—young and swept off her feet—and her only misfortune? Meeting a coercive controller/narcissistic abuser. She was perfect prey.*

When she was able to make her escape, Lily was able to access multiple high-level expert witnesses; however, her abuser was able to poke holes in her defense. This included having the coercive controller/narcissistic abuser's criminal charges of falsified college entrance applications not addressed in the family court. He used Lily's concerns about her child being complicit in the criminal activity to

turn this child against her and ultimately almost successfully her two younger children.

The indoctrination of the adult victim and that of the
children is similar and, like a cult and demonstrated by
Albert Biderman's research during the Korean war, victims are worn down and often acquiesce and even align
(Biderman, 1957). In 1973, Amnesty International's Report
on Torture stated that Biderman's Chart of Coercion contained the "universal tools of torture and coercion." Lily
was tortured and her children continue to be tortured. So
many children living under the "cult leader" and the "total-
itarianism" ruler are conditioned (brainwashed) into
aligning with this "leader." They have no choice—regardless if the leader, in this case a parent, is overtly abusive
or not. The children live in fear. Align or be punished. They
are no different than prisoners of war. It is an unacknowledged child abuse.

Parenting our children in the way that we planned is
sabotaged by the coercive controller/narcissistic abuser. In
the case of Lily, she wasn't allowed to parent at all. Lily
disengaged from the court system and stopped fighting for
what was rightfully hers, time with her children. Lily let
go of the rope. For her, she believes that letting go means
her children, the rope, may not be weaponized against the
abuser's target—her. She believes that by letting go of the
rope, there may be space for healing.

This may be the most painful decision a protective
mother could ever have to make, escaping the abuse by the
perpetrators, the ex-partner and the family court system,
knowing full well that her children are still living under the
coercive controller/narcissistic abuser's regime. But Lily

has hope that her boys are slowly yet assuredly continuing to gain clarity. The grief is immeasurable, but she is right there waiting for them when they are ready to step back into their mother's light.

— Dr. C

THE JUDGE'S NEW CLOTHES

Aurora's Story - Australia

I have a degree as an arts psychotherapist in sexual violence, domestic violence, coercive control, and trauma. I used to be a highly sought after therapist in Australia. I am an expert signatory for Amber Heard's Open Letter, which criticized her conviction on defamation charges and called for a great understanding of intimate partner violence.

I am also a mother who has had her child and parental rights removed due to the use of "parental alienation syndrome" accusations by the child's father. I am now an activist against parental alienation and a family law reformer due to this.

In 2009, I met a man who I now know to be a coercive controller/narcissistic abuser. Within the first hours of marriage, he displayed how he owned me. He began the physical abuse within one week of marriage, but I was too ashamed to leave, too ashamed to tell my friends. He said he would change and he said he would "help more" and look after a baby if we had one and not be abusive. I wanted to believe him. I was kidding myself. He would make me do everything. He diddled me out of the financial settlement of the house he forced me to clean and to pay for.

On the first anniversary of our wedding, we decided to "start again." We renewed our vows by ourselves. I even wore my wedding dress. Now I feel so much vulnerability for that me who was deluding herself and so wanted to believe. We conceived my daughter Laura that night.

Years later, after separation, when I went to get my belongings under police guard, he had secretly placed my wedding dress into a cupboard he knew I was collecting. He had thrown out every other single piece of my clothing I owned. The message was clear: You belong to me and you made a vow. He had always told me, "no one in my family ever gets divorced."

At the time, he pretended he was okay with the breakup, playing the helpless nice guy. But the post-separation domestic abuse was worse than I ever could have imagined. The moment I left the house with Laura to go live in a granny flat in my aunty and uncle's place, my daughter began displaying very strange behaviors after visiting with her father. She was two and a half years old.

From my education, I knew what was age appropriate and what was not. I knew how to redirect unhealthy behavior. But still, I was insecure and still being controlled by him. He would make me drive forty minutes at 4 a.m. to "his house" to wake him up for work at 5 a.m. when he had Laura. She would be in his bed without any underpants on, her hair smelling of his armpit. Asking him not to insist on Laura sleeping in his bed like this and for her to have her own bed got me a glass thrown at my face. It missed me by millimeters.

I wound up having to move back to the marital property. I saw him and his brother grooming Laura. I suddenly realized this was the answer to her strange behavior but could not say anything as he and his brother laughed and smiled in congratulations with each other at having achieved this "training" of Laura. I was by myself. The years of coercive control had told me that I was in danger if I raised this issue. So I took the blame. I said I was "paranoid" and needed Laura to sleep with me—in order to stop this. Unfortunately, this came back to bite me in family court.

Within three weeks of moving out again, Laura came home from a visit with what I believed to be signs of abuse. I was in shock and didn't know what to do. A doctor notified child safety. Police sent evidence to the DNA lab, which botched the evidence. This lack of testing stopped the investigation.

Her behavior had changed dramatically since that time and her day care caregivers noticed too. My daughter has disclosed for years since then. Child Safety (the child welfare agency in Australia) deemed me the protective parent, and he was only allowed supervised visitation. Laura's child psychologist said not to send her to a supervised contact center, so I insisted on going with her father to theme parks, parks, and beaches instead. I was so scared of him and so confused, with no advocacy services available and, with his story changing so often, I let him come whenever he wanted.

He refused to call Child Safety to "clear this up" as I asked him so many times. Because I did not want to supervise him. I didn't want this to be real. If I allowed him to have visits alone with Laura after Child Safety told me not to, she would be sent to foster care, and both I and my ex-husband would be investigated. I would be charged with child endangerment and neglect. He would tell me to "hand her over," he intimidated, verbally abused, manipulated, monitored, harassed, and stalked me. I thought I was supervising him when, in reality, he was monitoring me. In family court, he said he did this because he was still "in love" with me.

Eventually, he began confessing, as the child's sexual abuse disclosures could not be denied. She said "the monsters were touching her bum" and, as she continued going to therapy and felt safer, she began saying, "they put their penis inside her and it hurt." His story has changed no less than eight times. He was never shocked, never surprised by what she said. The police stated they believed us but could not get Laura to disclose it to them. Two child psychologists confirmed that Laura had been abused.

I cannot even begin to explain how traumatizing it is to witness your child's pain and listen to their disclosures. You are forced to become their therapist when all you want to do is be their mum. You document it, then you are accused of making it up in court.

Leaving my perpetrator was worse than staying with him. I have wished a thousand times I never left.

I was never believed by the courts, lawyers, or family court report writer, and least of all, the independent children's lawyer—the guardian ad litem (GAL). It all amounted to total destruction of my life, my child's life, and a complete removal of me as a mother in her life. He now has more control over me than ever before. I feel like my womb has been robbed.

My child will have the psychological damage of me taking her to the empty family courthouse and being told to wait for me at the child care facility. Then being removed by her father to live with him, never to see or speak to her mother again for over 90 days and never to return to her home, her community, belongings, and pets of seven years. All because of her lying and perpetrating father claimed "parental alienation." This was a father determined to be an unacceptable no-contact risk by the family court and the Magistrates Court of Australia for two years up until the day he took her.

The court order labeled me an unacceptable risk and psychological abuser. The order says that I made my child believe she had been sexually abused when she wasn't. This basically absolves the father of any sin—and it completely defames my character. Laura was sent to a parental reunification therapist to be told her mother is "sick in the head," in the words of a barrister.

He got to see thirty years' worth of treatment seeking case notes, the child's case notes, plus the police and child safety investigations via family court subpoenas. If he was in criminal court, this would never be allowed. The judgment relies on fantasy and perjury. My legally aided lawyer never showed up for trial. The paralegal that "represented" me was best friends with my ex-partner's lawyer, and the paralegal quit law the night of our last day of our trial.

The judgment is full of errors of fact. The judge made a finding of fact that domestic violence never existed because I sent him a text message once with a smiley face and that I was sex trafficked as a child. That I was "sexually projecting" onto my child because "anyone that has been sexually abused can make anyone around them think they have been sexually abused, just by being around them, especially children." This is what the family court report writer said because I was kidnapped and gang raped at seventeen. That his confessions were "coerced." That I never wanted my daughter. That Child Safety had never told me to do supervised visitation and that there was no DNA evidence.

The judge, lawyers, family court report writer, and independent children's lawyer relied on a false and malicious notification made by my sister, a Child Safety worker at the time, laid deliberately to help the father gain sole custody. No one in the court knew my sister had been arrested but not prosecuted and was sacked from her job for filing this false report. I only found out about it after trial. She had given the notification to the father. His affidavits and fabrications mirror the notification.

Although I proved that the father lied and the judgment had many errors during appeal, it was dismissed. The orders still stand. Again, I was failed by legal aid lawyers. The no-contact domestic violence order I put in place to protect myself and on which the child is named, is still active and is actually quite extensive. However, the judges of the Australian family law system are allowed to overrule these protective orders via their "discretion." They are not supposed to, and the law is changing to stop this.

The only way out for mothers and children in our situation in Australia is to file a "Rice & Asplund." This involves the mother going back to the court and telling them that she lied, she was crazy, delusional, and being vindictive so the father is innocent and did absolutely nothing wrong. The *Rice v. Asplund* case dealt with the living arrangements for a three-year-old child and established that, in order to get a modification, a parent had to prove there had been a significant change in circumstances since the final custody orders. The mother must go back to the family court and say that she lied about the sexual violence and everything else. That she has now "changed her ways." She must have psychiatric reports to prove this and she must be on medication. She must unequivocally state that she lied and she was of mistaken belief. If she says this, she may get some unsupervised visitation of her children but never proper custody ever again.

I have found out that, in the last ten years in Australia, every mother I have learned about that has been deemed a protective parent by child safety and then gone to family court to have their child protected—to gain sole custody—has lost all parental rights and physical custody.

Our orders are the exact "cure" for "alienators," as prescribed by Dr. Richard Gardner, the creator of the "parental alienation syndrome" legal abuse tactic. I have been ordered into two hours of supervised contact per fortnight for ten years, until she turns eighteen. I was her primary caregiver since birth.

Don't even get me started on the people who run "supervised contact centres" (which oversee visits with a noncustodial parent). They believe in parental alienation the most. Their businesses depend on it. And they are unaccredited and unregulated by the Australian government. I pay them a lot just to see my child, so it's in their best interest to keep me there.

I have come to liken "parental alienation syndrome" to the story of *The Emperor's New Clothes*. The judges parade around, ruling on this delusional ideology whilst the merchants, the lawyers, keep selling the invisible threads. They are quite literally weaving the cloth of parental alienation out of nothing. In the story, it is the children who point out that the emperor is wearing no clothing. It is the children who are now speaking out too.

Reversal of custody was the worst pain I have ever experienced in my entire life. Compounded with this injustice has been knowing the pain of my daughter. I have been so fortunate to be able to connect with other protective mothers around the world who are being subjected to the same thing. It makes me feel less insane.

I have come to learn that mothers who have been subjected to child removal are at very high risk of suicide and suicide ideation. And sadly, some others I know have died. I am now on disability support programs, and I get support workers every day to help me function. My mind is not what it used to be. I cannot work at capacity. I pay child support. Many women I know have children who blame their mothers after they age out. It hurts. I am preparing for it.

I am angry that the Australian government refuses to tell women that they may lose custody of their children for leaving their abuser and telling the police about it. I am fighting every single day for family law reform in Australia. I am so grateful for the support I get and the amazing advocates fighting for all these changes. I am sure parental alienation will not stand the test of time. The tide is turning.

Since my daughter was taken, I have contacted thirty-three lawyers, including three community legal services. None of them will represent me. All of them say that it is out of their expertise. One even said she wouldn't take it on if I had a million dollars. My ex has not stopped breaching the orders, beginning within twenty-four hours of him having custody of her. He has violated the orders over fifty times. He monitors our one-per-fortnight video calls and does not give her all the gifts I send. He refuses to answer my correspondence, and he has not delivered her for contact for seven months. I am "pro se," or self-represented, as many mothers in my situation are.

I long for the day my daughter comes home. I pray constantly for it. Thank you for giving me the opportunity to write this and have it published. Just writing

it to you, knowing you believe me, makes such a dif-
ference.

NOTES

In October 2023, the Australian Parliament passed the Family Law Amendment Act and the Family Law Amendment (Information Sharing) Act. These represent major legal changes about how Australian courts make parenting decisions in the best interests of a child. The laws took effect on May 6, 2024, and repealed a legal presumption introduced in 2006 stating it was in the best interest of children for parents to have "equal shared parental responsibility." Fathers' rights groups pushed for this equal custody law but, in cases where there was domestic abuse, children were put in danger.

As we see all over the world, many of these unfortunate custody decisions come down to how judges are trained and influenced. In Australia, this presumption led judges to believe equal parenting time was good for children. And, even though there were always exceptions for domestic violence, the overriding belief in shared custody led to decisions that overlooked patterns of abuse. As a result, abuse victims were reluctant to bring these matters up in court—for fear they would be labeled as an obstructionist or alienator. Here's just one family cited in the Parliament of New South Wales's report, Child Protection and Social Services System, *published in 2022:*

> *"Case study: The Edwards family Inquiry participants discussed the case of Sydney teenagers*

Jack and Jennifer Edwards, who were shot and killed by their estranged father, John Edwards, in 2018. John Edwards had a long history of violence towards his domestic partners and children. Jack and Jennifer's mother, Olga Edwards, took her own life five months after the murder of her children. A 2020 coronial inquest found that significant failings by the independent children's lawyer (ICL) appointed to represent Jack and Jennifer led to the Court ordering weekly contact arrangements with their father. This was in clear opposition to the children's wishes and placed them at risk of harm."

Some of the new factors Australian judges are directed to consider when awarding custody are: the views of the child, their psychological and developmental needs, the safety of the child and their caregivers, the capacity of each parent to provide for the child's needs, and the benefit to the child of having a relationship with each of their parents.

— Amy Polacko

THE ACCUSATION IS THE CONFESSION

Angela's Story - United States

loved that our similarities were the strengths of our early relationship; our respective parents and grandparents came from humble, immigrant backgrounds and were seeking a more fruitful life in the United States. Education and work ethic were valued as the pathway to a successful and stable life. I thought we were both interested in finishing our respective graduate school degrees, starting careers, and becoming financially stable while building a family. We got to know each other's friends and grew a tight-knit community from these people and colleagues too. I believed that, in Steve, I had a partner with similar goals and values. After five years, he finished his law degree and worked at a stable law firm. We decided to get married, buy a home, and start a family. I was still completing my training program as a doctor and was pulling only a base salary. However, with both of us gainfully employed, I felt we were in a good position to accomplish our goals as long as we continued to live modestly.

The reality is I didn't know the financial state of affairs we were living in. Just weeks before our first child was born, Steve dropped the bombshell that he was quitting his job with the law firm and starting his own practice. I felt nauseated and overwhelmed and feared what the financial risk and instability would bring. It felt foreboding almost like my body knew intuitively what lay ahead. This is probably because I was aware of the significant debt Steve accrued from two mortgages he was carrying on condominiums he purchased. This should have been a red flag. The condos were in disrepair and became uninhabitable due to his lack of upkeep. Now this change in his career. I was distraught yet unable to express my fears about the financial burdens we were carrying. I knew he would become angry, so I remained silent and accepted his decision. I would later find out that he had defaulted on student loans I thought were in forbearance.

With an infant son and blindsided by the financial mess we were in, I felt a tremendous amount of anxiety and stress about not being able to pay our household bills. Additionally, I was paying for Steve's mother's living expenses while she cared for our baby. This included paying for my mother-in-law's rent and utilities. I realize now that he coerced me into doing this, reducing me to begging Steve every month to contribute to his share of the required household bills. It was impossible to make ends meet with these burdens. I was also coerced into shouldering more loans, which he insisted we both take to renovate the home we had purchased. This first year of marriage, a new baby, and a new home, I should have been happy. Yet I felt betrayed and alone. I had not expected to be living under such financial duress.

In this early part of the marriage, I had the clarity early on that I know so many victims and survivors wish they had. The involvement of Steve's mother in our personal affairs made for a great deal of triangulation. I felt myself shrinking away. I began to realize my partner was actually not the person I thought he was, and I became desperate for a divorce. I made this intention clear to Steve. Anytime I broached the subject, he would tell me divorce was not an option and threatened that if I tried to leave him, he would take our son away from me. Of course, like so many victims and survivors, I could not believe that he actually could mean this—that he would take our child away from me. But the intimidation worked. And so did the intermittent reinforcement. I held on to the "breadcrumbs" when Steve told me he loved me and that he wanted better for our family. It didn't help that I was isolated, since my family was not nearby. A child, no savings, significant debt, and the added stress of an intense training program I needed to finish to become a licensed doctor. I felt trapped. Deep down, I knew it would get worse if I left.

In the meantime, I also became aware of a source of income that Steve was hiding in his mother's name. Now I understood why he would wait until I exhausted all of my financial resources for monthly bills before he would supplement it. It was all about control. I realized that this power dynamic would never end. His goal was to keep me financially entrenched so that when we eventually divorced, he would be entitled to half of everything and still have this resource of hidden money. I was devastated. It was not just the money, but the secrets, lies, and deception that went along with him enjoying the financial security of having family money at his disposal while leaving me exposed and financially responsible for so much accruing debt. I begged him to cut back on spending, to ease the overwhelming burden I felt from living financially underwater. Steve refused. And then he dropped another bombshell, unilaterally deciding that he would give up his law practice and go to business school for an MBA. There was no use fighting this. He was going to do this no matter how I objected, and I was expected to support him and move to a smaller house to cut back on acquired expenses.

At the time, his credit score was horrible, and I knew he would not qualify for graduate school loans without a co-signer. For the longest time, I thought his mother was in on this because she cosigned his loans. I now know he was controlling her finances also and using her to gain assets. This is yet another example of his using others for his own gain—even his own mother. I was trying to stay afloat, working full time in a rigorous program, caring for our child, along with serving as the primary home manager. I was exhausted. He was intentionally wearing me down.

Every victim has a moment—an incident that creates the awareness that staying is no longer an option. In year six of the marriage, there was "that" incident. The finances had not changed, with financial duress evident. We owed the preschool my son attended $10,000. I could never imagine the lengths Steve would go to avoid paying the bill. He poisoned our then five-year-old with hand sanitizer. Steve then blamed the poisoning on our child's preschool teachers, stating that they had made him ingest the hand sanitizer. I feared that if he so blatantly endangered our son's life, he would do it again and possibly kill me or our daughter, who was a toddler at that time. I knew all of our lives were in danger. I filed for divorce.

All those threats about taking our children away? They were not idle. Steve went straight to court and secured an ex parte restraining order against me, forcing me to leave my home and my children behind. This would not be the first time he did this. I could not eat or go to work due to the shock. I lost fifteen pounds in the ten days I had to wait before I saw my kids again. And then, what I know now is so predictable with these coercively controlling men, revenge became his goal. The weaponization of what matters most to me, my children, became his strategy via legal abuse. No one could have prepared me for the onslaught from this attorney who is the father of my children.

He filed false restraining orders against me, presenting false accusations to court officials, interfering with the children's therapy, and, of course, saturating them with falsehoods about me being an unfit parent.

He told them, "Mom is not invested in your receiving a quality education," "Mom is trying to get you infected with COVID," and "Mom wants to kidnap you and take you out of state." All of his accusations toward me were actually his confessions. Little did I know that it was he who would eventually kidnap my children and move them out of state! He also told my children that they were unsafe with me and that I could not be trusted, explaining that this was due to "mental illness" that runs in my family. He was specific: telling them that when I become upset, my behavior escalates and I would eventually hurt them. The children slowly began to believe him. They would see that I was reasonably upset by the ongoing events and believed more and more that I was unstable, might kidnap them, or could harm them. Any effort I made to reassure them that I was safe and wanted to let the professionals in our case decide what was in their best interest, went unnoticed.

Then he did what I could never have predicted. On one of my visits with my children, I had reserved time at a hotel so we could enjoy time by a pool. He called the police saying I was kidnapping the children and coerced my son to call the police explaining that he felt unsafe and that I was kidnapping the children. This on the heels of the Department of Children and Families (DCF) making an unannounced visit to my home—catching me and my children off guard. Mind you, unannounced visits are welfare checks for children in danger. My son had a panic attack. DCF confirmed that my children were safe in my care and that my son's reactions were directly related to their investigation of my home. But my abuser capitalized on this—instilling more fear in my children—explaining that DCF only makes visits to homes that are unsafe. DCF didn't protect my children; they emboldened a harmful parent. I know this happens to many protective parents.

Eventually, Steve kidnapped the children. He had been building toward this all along, taking the children to interview at schools out of state, lying about residency, and then enrolling them in school all without my consent. He then moved them, relocating our children without a court order. The family court did nothing to stop this or to return my children back to the state where we had started our family.

The system allowed Steve to take complete control of our lives and virtually erase me from the lives of my children. And the sad part is that it wasn't very challenging for him to do. Unlike some stories I hear, I was never deemed an unfit parent. All of his allegations were dismissed. I'm sure him being a lawyer was useful. Steve sued three of my past lawyers, the guardian ad litem, and custody evaluators also. No doubt, they became more passive, fearing his retaliation. The length of time it took for each court proceeding, and subsequent investigations, gave Steve what he needed to cement his plan to erase me. Their integration into a new school and community and limited contact with me, due to his blocking visitation for a span of about three years, left the court to dismiss his violations. His manipulation of the system, and the fact that the system did not recognize his intentions to harm me and subsequently my children, sometimes is the most significant betrayal.

The trauma our children carry is the most overwhelming aspect of the grief. I know my children didn't ask for this and that they have been coerced into compliance. After the first ex parte, my daughter, four years old, told me she was looking all over the house for me and even in the stream in the backyard. She became behaviorally dysregulated at school and the teachers had to send her home, as they were unable to keep her safe at school.

I am still mostly estranged from my children and only see them for lunch twice a month. The emotional devastation at times feels unbearable, but I have learned to cope with the help of my family and spiritual and social support from friends and colleagues. With protective parenting techniques, I have been able to diffuse a lot of the toxicity they bring to our visits and try to build back as many positive interactions as possible. I am doing the best that I can in the most horrifying of circumstances. I can only hope that as they continue to move on in their own lives and gain freedom from our abuser, that they will gain clarity and agency and return to my loving arms.

NOTES

In Angela's story, we can see that the threats are never idle and that the system becomes complicit in the harm. The coercive controller/narcissistic abuser literally accused her of everything he was doing to her—DARVOing her—

and robbed her children of their formative years with their loving protective mother. This is common among protective mothers, as you will notice in the stories read here. Perpetrators will claim victim status, denying any wrongdoing and reversing victim and offender (DARVO), a term created by Dr. Jennifer Freyd (1997).

Angela's recourse is minimal because as we know all too well judicial immunity prevails. As Stephens and colleagues found in their research (2022), family court often seems to deviate from what is supposed to be its primary mission, supporting families through what are already challenging experiences. Situations all too often become worse when family court is brought on the scene.

Stories like this, and all the others in this book, make those of us advocating for protective parents furious with a system that fails to recognize the harmful character traits of these disordered abusers. This father outwitted the family court system and did so blatantly, without any repercussions. A bully who's able to intimidate court professionals and therapists and willing to do anything to harm the protective parent, including kidnap Angela's children. All of this, and he walked away scot-free.

The indoctrination of the children started early on, and the coercive controller/narcissistic abuse continues to work toward fracturing their attachment with Angela. But Angela's superpower is her ability to take the little time she has with her children to continue to reignite and strengthen their attachment with her. In the end, her children will see her for who she really is— the amazing loving mother they have always known.

—Dr. C

CONGRATS! YOU LOST CUSTODY

Charlotte's Story – United States

S hortly after graduating from college, I accepted my first teaching job. A few months later, I met Mike through a coworker who had previously dated him. There were red flags everywhere, including his alcohol addiction. Mike was also dishonest frequently, telling small little lies that piled up. I knew something didn't feel right, and my parents also expressed concerns.

Despite all of this, I was ready to settle down and have a family, so I chose to overlook these red flags. I focused on his good qualities, and in the beginning, there were many.

We became engaged and were married within two years. We had our first child, Elizabeth, eighteen months later. When she was three months old, Mike and I separated due to his alcohol abuse. He threatened to hurt me and to murder me if I decided to leave him. I knew the threats were real so, like so many victims, I relented and decided to try marriage counseling. At

the same time, Mike started seeing an addiction counselor.

Victims are known to rationalize bad behaviors and
to disassociate. I was no different. I remained hopeful that things would improve. Perhaps Mike's threats
were just in moments of anger and alcohol use? He
promised he would stop his excessive drinking. For a
while, things seemed to be better. When I gave birth to
our second child, Alexander, I could see Mike slipping
back into his old patterns. This time, he tried to hide
his excessive drinking, but it was nearly impossible for
him to do so.

I left and returned multiple times. I kept thinking
that it was best for the children to have their father in
their life and for us to be a family. Each time things
improved, even if just slightly, I committed fully. This
time was no different, and before I knew it, we were
having our third child, Katherine. Mike, just like each
time before, became more abusive and his alcohol
abuse intensified.

Finally, after finding an open bottle of vodka in his
car and catching him multiple times secretly drinking
in the yard and in the garage, I gave him an ultimatum.
He agreed to stop drinking entirely and even signed an
agreement that stated if he relapsed, I would have full
custody of the children.

Not surprisingly, the drinking returned and was
worse than before. Mike was driving under the influence and was engaging in neglectful parenting, behaving in frightening ways while intoxicated. I knew the
kids were in danger and we had to leave. And then he

did the unthinkable: he dropped our two-year-old, breaking her arm. Two weeks later, I filed for divorce. However, this is not the worst part of the story. Mike is an alcoholic, but first and foremost, he is an abuser.

The gaslighting began immediately. Mike claimed I had conjured up all these stories of his drinking and neglectful harmful behaviors. He told me and everyone he knew that I was crazy, that no one would love me, and he threatened me as he did that very first time—that if I followed through with the divorce, he would kill me, or worse, he would get 50-50 custody. He knew my biggest fear was leaving the children in his care. He knew how much I loved taking care of them and wanted to be at home with them. He told me he would make sure that I had to work full time, forcing our children into daycare.

Thankfully, I had documented all the alcohol abuse and the judge in our divorce case agreed that Mike needed to have supervised visitation with the children. Mike's sisters were assigned as supervisors. The judge ordered Mike to complete a breathalyzer test before visitation and every four hours during the visit. Multiple times he had positive results and would skip tests, and our children reported that they saw both of his twin sisters taking the breathalyzer test for him. Eventually, we were assigned a new family court judge, and this judge didn't have any concerns about Mike's alcohol abuse. Mike was granted unsupervised visits.

It's hard to imagine, but the children seemed to be coping okay under the circumstances, although they reported that Mike was drunk at every custodial time, which was now including overnights. Elizabeth, our oldest, was now seven and would share with me how she was making dinner for everyone while at her dad's house, finding what she could in the pantry, preparing and packing lunches, and getting her younger siblings their clothes ready for school the next day.

I thought it couldn't get any worse. Yet soon both of my girls alleged that their paternal grandmother was molesting them while they sat on her lap, and then all three of my children disclosed that their father's cousin was "doing things" to them. The children disclosed that their father witnessed the cousin abusing them, but in court their father lied and stated that the children had never been alone with their cousin. I could not change the visitation plan. The court did not see the urgency of this matter.

About a year later, the children revealed that their father was also molesting them at night. Mike had confided in me that he had been sexually abused as a child by a babysitter, but my suspicion was always that his mother was the one who had molested him while his father was deployed or gone for extended periods attending college six hours away. Mike had disclosed to me that his maternal grandfather had a serious problem with alcohol and pornography, often watching it in the presence of the entire family during holiday gatherings. I began to see that this is a multigenerational problem. But I was literally trapped. I had no way to protect my kids from the abuse.

Each time they reported another assault, the Tennessee Department of Children's Services (DCS) would investigate and then quickly unsubstantiate the cases. There were over twenty-four reports to DCS. Only two of them were made by me. My children were forced back into the care of their abusers—not one abuser—but several that lived in that home. They knew they were disbelieved by DCS and this affirmed what they were being told by their abusers: no one would believe them, and if they kept it up—kept reporting abuse—they would never see me again because I would go to jail. My oldest eventually gave up talking about the abuse. She became their "favorite" and was given more freedom at their father's home. My youngest two spent hours in their room "punished" for continuing to disclose.

From the very beginning of the divorce proceedings, Mike continually stalled the process and did not comply with court orders. My attorney was forced to file dozens of motions, yet Mike still didn't actually submit his financials and other assets until about eighteen months after the divorce. Mike wouldn't give me access to my belongings in the home, and the threats and intimidation were never-ending. He was stalking me and bold enough to let me know that he knew my location all the time. He assumed he was above the law and sent me incessant emails, text messages, and phone calls making physical threats and telling me that I would lose custody of the children.

I filed a police report that resulted in an order of protection. Less than six months later, the second police report resulted in our new family court judge pulling that criminal complaint back into the civil court and treating it as part of a "high-conflict" custody battle. He issued a joint restraining order, even though Mike hadn't asked for one. It was obvious this new judge was more interested in protecting Mike than me or the children. I was given a stern warning: If I kept bringing these "baseless" abuse allegations to his courtroom, he would be forced to severely restrict my contact with the children.

Mike refused to sign the final divorce decree for five months and on the same day he signed it, he filed for a change in custody. I had nine witnesses testifying for the children, photographs illustrating the abuse he had wielded on the kids, and all the threatening texts and emails from him. A week after the last day of the four-day custody trial, Mike was arrested for child endangerment after my oldest child, the "favorite," called 911 because her dad was drunk and threatening her and her siblings.

When the police arrived at the house, Mike refused to open the door so they broke his door down. Our family court judge had evidence of this incident yet still designated Mike as primary parent with school and medical decision-making. I was being punished for trying to protect my children. The judge actually blamed me for Mike's excessive drinking, saying he was "understandably stressed by all of the court pro-ceedings."

Additionally, the fact that DCS had closed the more than two-dozen investigations into the abuse of my children was enough for the judge to deem me as a vin-dictive ex-wife who would stop at nothing to keep the children from having a relationship with their father. This judge pointed out several times in his written decision that he was thankful he had been able to observe my demeanor. This statement alone would make it difficult for his decision to be overturned on appeal. The judge further defended his conclusion by claiming I had somehow been able to convince every witness, including the court-appointed forensic psychologist, court-appointed child therapist, my children's pediatrician, three teachers, two school counselors, and a police officer to have a negative opinion of Mike. I was ordered to pay $50,000 of my ex's attorney fees. As a first-grade teacher, I barely earned that much in an entire year, forcing me to file for bankruptcy.

Since I had supposedly done so many egregious things—for example, attempted to protect my children from their abusive father and his abusive family members—I needed to be punished. The judge remanded me to spend six days in jail (at the height of the COVID pandemic) for withholding my children from their father. Finally, the worst of this was that I was not allowed to have any contact with my children for five weeks. I was devastated. There was no way to know if my children were okay, and of course, there was no way to prevent the abuse from occurring.

My attorney filed an appeal, but as expected, the appeals court completely agreed with the trial court's findings. The case was all over the internet and the oral arguments were published on YouTube. I even received a bright yellow "Congratulations—You Did It" award from a large law practice four hours away for "losing custody and decision-making." They posted it on their website.

My children and I were shattered. We had long ago lost faith that anyone would protect them, but we could not have predicted this mockery of our situation. But my brave six-year-old would not be silenced.

Less than six months after the appellate court published their decision and only three months after the family court judge officially closed the case, my six-year-old wrote a letter to her teacher about the sexual abuse she was suffering at the hands of her father. As a mandated reporter, the DCS investigation was reopened. This time, after the kids completed their fifth forensic interview, their father's rights to unsupervised visitation were removed. Over time, every visitation supervisor, including the children's grandmother and a few different friends, were forbidden to supervise visits with the children anymore. I was grateful that the family court judge had closed that case prior to this investigation because it sent jurisdiction to the juvenile court.

A guardian ad litem (GAL) was appointed, and the state filed dependency and neglect charges against my ex. Probable cause was found, and an adjudicatory trial was set. There were months of delays, but on the morning of the first day DCS and a therapist testified. After the lunch break, Mike offered to give up his parental rights in exchange for the juvenile court case being closed. I was in disbelief and cautiously optimistic. Then several weeks later, Mike rescinded his offer, causing the trial to be backed up another six months.

On the first day of the second trial, the children (then seven, nine, and eleven) testified as well as a second therapist. Following that day, Mike signed papers that he would be moving forward with relinquishing his rights rather than being formally charged by the district attorney with molesting his own children. He had multiple stipulations, but we didn't blink an eye and immediately agreed to everything. It took another fourteen months for the documents to be finalized. The overwhelming trauma experienced by all of us, further inflicted by a court system that took fourteen months to finalize the order, cannot be understated. Thankfully, my children are now safe. They have since been adopted by my husband and are healing and experiencing a life without abuse for the first time.

My case cost more than $400,000 in attorneys' fees, psychological evaluations, and therapy. There will more than likely be thousands more needed for the ongoing therapy my children will need to heal. The worst part is none of this needed to happen. The evidence was always there, but the family court was more intent on supporting an abusive father than protecting my children.

NOTES

Himpathy. Kate Manne coined this term defining it as the shaper of misogyny. Her book Down Girl *explains the logic of misogyny, not simply "men who hate women" but a far-reaching punitive social system that keeps women in their place by rewarding compliance and punishing resis-*

tance (2018). Extending the term himpathy *to the family court gives us context for Charlotte's story and each story in this book. Imagine trying to protect your children from an abusive parent only to be remanded to jail? As we read in the preface and in other stories in this book, family courts are a "lawless land." And as if it wasn't bad enough for Charlotte to be jailed for protecting her children, imagine a law firm posting a congratulations certificate for losing custody of her children? The callous disregard for the trauma experienced by Charlotte was bad enough, but to make a mockery of what her children experienced? Unthinkable.*

Additionally, research affirms that coercive controllers/ narcissistic abusers avoid taking responsibility and that the court will hold someone else responsible (Rosenfeld et al. 2019). It's easier to hold victims responsible in a world where, as Dr. Lisa Fontes, an expert in coercive control, states, "entire belief systems enshrine men's control over women" (2015, 67). Attorneys and other court professionals who fail to recognize and manage these individuals with harmful character traits are simply less able to meet their ethical obligations and to advocate for victims-survivors. It's apparent there may be a desensitization that occurs, creating less accountability by the attorneys and the systems themselves. The overwhelming grief is when a victim-survivor knows full well that the evidence was clear and that, as with Charlotte, the system chose not to protect.

As Dr. Emma Katz (2022) states, "grossly unequal expectations are implicitly placed on mothers and fathers/ father figures" (30). Mothers are expected to live in these oppressive circumstances in silence, and if they finally gain the courage to escape, they know that their children will be forced to have contact with the coercive controller/narcissistic abuser. In the case of Charlotte, she couldn't protect her children from child predators.

— Dr. C

800 DAYS AND COUNTING

Stephanie's Story - United States

T here is an old adage that is founded upon scripture: "Evil prevails when the good do nothing." My story starts with the present day.

How did I arrive at this present day under these conditions that contain days upon days of suffering at the hands of others? It began in 1985. I was fifteen years old when I met the coercive controller/narcissistic abuser, the man that I ended up marrying. I look back now and wish that I had seen the red flags and the signs that are now becoming more commonly known.

We began dating in high school. He always had excuses and reasons why we could not go to his house. It took six months before he told me that he didn't live in the school district we were attending and was using his stepmother's mom's address as his residence (his grand-stepmother). This is when the lying began, and it never ended. At age fifteen, he already had aced the skill set of these coercive controllers/narcissistic abusers. The psychological warfare was all a game. At my age, I did not know that this level of liar existed in the world. It was not that I was sheltered, but more so that I believed in the best of people and that someone who "loved" me would not seek to deceive me to this level.

Fast forward through thirty-two years of life and sixteen years of marriage. I was left feeling like I was caught in a wave, rolling toward shore where I could never find "up" or breathable air. Where I was always to blame for everything in our marriage, I could do no right, and I was controlled at almost every corner without even realizing it. I was a stay-at-home mom, a requirement by Kyle for ten years after the birth of our first child—even though I had six years of college education that included a master's degree. I should have known then that the children were simply an object for him, and that he had no interest in parenting them or participating in their day-to-day routines.

Our marriage was tumultuous, and in between the births of our third and fourth children, my husband moved out of our marital home. I was relieved yet wounded. It wasn't until a year and a half after our divorce that I would come to discover that he wasn't "couch surfing" as he told me, but had rented a four-bedroom suburbia home and moved in with another woman and her son while we were still married. We had three children at the time—ages nine, four, and two.

In the seventeenth year of our marriage, Kyle stopped providing any income for our family. Our youngest child had been born only a month and a half prior. Though I had a position with a start-up technology company that I had secured only a few months before the birth of our last child, it was not enough for me to support our four children, ages one, three, five, and ten at the time, and our monthly housing expenses. Within four months, the children and I lost the home that we had lived in for seven years. We were forced with the decision to either go to a homeless shelter or live in the rented home that my husband had shared with his mistress and her son for a year. But, at the time, I was not aware a mistress even existed.

We lived with him for seven weeks. It was hell on earth. His goal was to torment me and my children in multiple ways, including to try to force me to agree to sign a document that said that I didn't need child or spousal support. Living in this rented home ended when Kyle pressed false charges—accusing me of domestic violence. Over a year later, I would learn that he filed the domestic violence charges against me on the exact *same day* that he had filed domestic violence charges against his former mistress two years before. Coincidence? I think not.

The children and I moved into a hotel. Kyle wanted the judge to take the children away from me and, when this did not occur, he filed false claims that I threw the children down the stairs. This would prove to be the first of five times that my abusive ex-husband falsified information and had my children taken from me.

There are no words to describe my shock and overwhelming grief when my children were stolen from me. We have missed birthdays, Christmases, Easters, church services, family vacations, walks in the park, and I have missed normal mothering that every mother assumes she will have— helping my children with homework, attending soccer games, and enjoying the warmth of the hugs we shared. The losses are too long to count—the list would span more than 800 days.

To be clear, to accomplish this theft, an orchestration of people was needed with one goal in mind—to protect their own vested interests—with no regard for the physical safety and psychological welfare of my children. I am doing what any protective mother would do. I am trying to figure out a way to receive justice, and more importantly, to return my children back to my care, to their loving protective mother.

As of this writing, I have lived almost twenty-four months without visitation with my children. They were removed from my care in May of 2022. In the last eleven years, there have been five times that my children have been taken from me, based solely upon corruption in our county's family court system. During most of those periods of time, not only visitation but any contact with my children has been cut off. In our county, magistrates are assigned to the case by the judge. Magistrates sit on the cases for the duration of the case, and the judge only needs to weigh in if there are questions specific to the case. Magistrates serve at the pleasure of the judge.

I have never been abusive. But I attempted to escape an abusive relationship. I couldn't have imagined the power my ex, Kyle, had to wield over me and that the family court system would be his proxy to do so. I couldn't have imagined that things could get worse.

Yet, in May of 2022, I was removed as custodial parent of my children with a no-visitation order. I was only allowed to communicate with my children via telephone and participate in parenting from afar, attending school and extracurricular activities.

There is no doubt that this was retaliation for the affidavit of disqualification against the judge that I filed in April 2022 with the state's chief justice of our supreme court. For over nine years, the magistrate in our case had consistently ignored blatant abuse by my ex and any disclosures of abuse made by the children. These included our oldest daughter, at ten, reporting her fear of her father to her school guidance counselor and to law enforcement. There have been substantiated child protective services reports and forensic evaluations all affirming my children's words—yet the guardian ad litem has done nothing to protect them and has perjured herself on the stand— denying these substantiated reports of abuse.

In April 2022, just days before filing the affidavit of disqualification, I filed a motion of special damage and emergency custody, requesting that the judge overseeing our case report the violations of law and ethics specific to the egregious actions by the magistrate and guardian ad litem on the case to the disciplinary counsel of the state. As the overseeing judge of the domestic relations court in our county, he is a mandatory reporter to the disciplinary counsel. The result: eleven days later, this order.

Mind you, this May order was made by an interim magistrate—a person serving for one day on our case.

How is it that she was able to strip me of my custodial time with a day on the case? How did she create a ruling and a temporary order without ever having a full hearing? Because she too was a participant in the family court ordered judicial abuse, and the best interest of my children was not on her list of priorities as a magistrate in this court. She too was complicit in family court–ordered trauma.

There is no judicial oversight. There is judicial impunity. I was deemed "dangerous" for attempting to request an independent investigation into violations of criminal law (perjury) and violations of ethics committed by people who hold licenses to practice law in our state.

It took seventeen months from the time of the magistrate's decision in January 2022 to receive a response from the judge on our objections. That judgment entry finally came in July 2023, and my ex was given full custody. I received supervised parenting time, and the parenting coordinator was given full discretion on this parenting time.

Legal counsel explained that an appeal could take a year and half to be heard, so at their advice, I filed another motion for full legal custody in August 2023. We did this knowing full well that, unfortunately, the original magistrate who I had filed the affidavit of disqualification to the judge against was reinstated back on our case. I knew our case would be wrought with injustice by a biased and vindictive magistrate.

At the end of December 2023, we filed a pretrial motion that contained information and evidence of child abuse and child neglect, which denotes a change in circumstance in our state. We had also reported child abuse and child neglect to the guardian ad litem in an extensive email in mid-December 2023. Over the years, we have repeatedly reported the child abuse and child neglect to the GAL. It is abundantly clear that her only motive has been to protect the abuser.

In January 2024, my children and I had still not had regular visitation since May of 2022. How can this not be the most heinous crime? At a pretrial hearing, the vindictive magistrate furthered the judicial abuse in act of hate toward me, and without any evidentiary hearing, trial, evidence, facts, or witnesses, she created a no-contact order against me with my children: "This prohibited contact includes direct contact, all written communication, all telephone communication, all communication through social media [such as texting, e-mail, Facebook, etc.] and any and all indirect communication through third parties including, but not limited to, her [my present] husband." The magistrate forbade me access to any records related to my children, including school, medical, mental health, and otherwise, and also forbade me from attending any school or extracurricular activities. Reading this, you might think I am a criminal. At the very least, a seriously bad, mentally unstable mother. By February of 2024, without any hearing or even a motion before the court, these orders were made "permanent."

In the two weeks that I had a civil protection order (CPO) against me and was unable to see my children, I rented a condo and quickly established a home for the children. I was forced to give up additional child visitation to my ex-husband in exchange for him dropping the false claims that led to the CPO.

During these two weeks, he told our second oldest child, our daughter who was five years old at the time, that I had been killed in a car accident.

The crimes against our family have continued to the present day and left us with few measures to overcome what has happened to our family. We have contacted local law enforcement, federal law enforcement, congressmen for our state, state senators for our district, the attorney general, children's services, and the disciplinary counsel. Though we have been unsuccessful in getting anyone to investigate, there are measures left to continue the fight. And we will continue to fight as our children ask most days, "How long, momma, how long until I get out and this is over?"

It's obvious I am being punished for the filing of the affidavit of disqualification. The reality is that my children have been punished all along. Their abuse— since the divorce process started —entirely ignored. The magistrate is ruling from a foundation of hate. She believes, and rightfully so, that I am trying to have her removed. She is using her pen and paper to attack me and harm my children. She believes that she is above the law—and it continues to be proven that she is.

The judge is no better. The last time we filed a motion to object to the magistrate's decision, he waited eighteen months to respond. I filed another motion to object to the magistrate's decision and know that it could be another eighteen months, or even five years, before we get a ruling from the judge. There are no time limits for when a judge has to rule. Can you imagine? Children living with an abuser and the family court judge has no time constraints in making a final decision for their safety? Magistrates apparently have carte blanche in rulings, and in this case, denying the psychological and physical well-being of my children.

Since I have lost so much, there seems little else that could be taken from me. People from our community are in the next steps of planning to seek a citizen impeachment—an attempt to impeach the judge on this case using a provision of our state's constitution that will allow us to take this action. It will require the signatures of 15 percent of the registered voters in our county. That percentage equates to 23,000 signatures. I do not believe this is an effort pursued before, and I am hopeful since it is literally the only accountability that there may be for the harms inflicted on my children by a complicit court system and their coercively controlling father.

Stay tuned.

NOTES

If he were a stranger, his behavior would be considered criminal, yet only in family court can an abuser get away with crimes against his own family.

Stephanie believed at her core that justice would have to be served, that her attempts to protect her children from abuse—from the person that abused her—would be heard and that she and her children would be protected.

And when that didn't happen, she did what any protective mother on the planet would be expected to do: she called out the egregious injustice. And then she learned, as so many of these stories illustrate, that judicial immunity permeates the system.

Stephanie, like so many mothers who have attempted to stand up to complicit family court "actors," was punished. A magistrate, behaving much like the coercive controller/ narcissistic abuser, became intent on revenge. The judge in this case did nothing to prevent this from occurring, allowing the children to be placed in the abuser's custody.

How dare a protective mother question a judge, a guardian ad litem, a custody evaluator, or, as was the case here, a magistrate's decision? How dare a protective mother be distraught over a decision and challenge this decision?

Lest you think this seems implausible, it is not. These occurrences happen day after day in family court. Judicial immunity shields judges from civil liability for judicial acts. Judicial immunity, dating back to a 1607 English case, is broad and it covers: (1) "judicial acts" that are (2) not undertaken in "clear absence of all jurisdiction." Assuming a judge does not run afoul of these two conditions, a judge cannot be civilly liable —even if the judge acts maliciously or corruptly (Harvard Law Review 2023, 1460–1461).

—Dr. C

GOD'S PLAN

Sarah's Story - United States

My only crime is that of being a mother. My story begins in my senior year of high school, but, perhaps, earlier than that. I grew up in a broken home, a product of divorce who never saw the love between a man and a woman. Growing up, I wanted so badly to be loved and to feel love. Not to mention, I was extremely sensitive and had an infectious smile and deep admiration and love for people.

In high school, you could find me volunteering in foreign countries or campaigning for environmental changes to save the rainforest. I believed that goodness exists in every single person and that everyone was deserving of love. I was ripe to fall for someone who disguised love with abuse.

I remember my eyes first catching his. Stan was different from anyone I had known. His piercing brown eyes, love of salsa music, and his disadvantaged upbringing made me fall hard. I was completely swept away and made to feel like I was his "reina," or queen, with never-ending handwritten notes professing his love for me and enough bouquets of flowers to fill up a football field. I was his "soulmate" and nothing would break us apart. My Disney fairy-tale ending seemed to be coming true.

Our story wasn't always a bed of roses or sweet notes of love. Darkness and abuse lurked at almost every corner. Yet Stan had the ability to crack me open in a way no one had before. After sharing how he was abused as a young child, I responded by sharing that he wasn't alone and that I too had been victimized. It was on a cool winter day, sitting on a bench, when I opened up and shared my dark childhood secret. Stan responded in love, holding my hand, wiping my tears away, and telling me he loved me the same and would help me. A short while later, I found myself in a vulnerable and compromising situation and again heard those words repeated, "This will help you. I can heal you."

He had planned a "surprise date" and told me to be ready by 7 o'clock. I got into his small, blue car and listened to the local radio station playing Christina Aguilera's and Britney Spears's latest hits as we drove for close to an hour. When we finally arrived, all I could see was an empty field surrounded by pine trees. Off in the distance was a metal fence and bright spotlights. The sounds of airplane engines were close by. I thought he took me to watch turbo jets take off and land at the nearby international airport. For a few minutes, we sat in the dark inside his car, listening and watching the powerful forces of nature take off and land, and then the "real surprise" started.

He pulled me close, started to kiss me, and put his hand up my blouse. I reminded him that I was not ready and that I had made a promise to myself and to God that I wanted to wait until marriage. His response still haunts me today. "I can heal you. I can help you. Let me do these things so you are no longer a prude. Trust me." I remember pushing his head away as he forced himself in between my legs and telling him "no, please." He ignored me. Tears streamed down my face as I said again, "please, no." Stan moaned in pleasure in my pain. At that moment, I felt paralyzed for the first of many moments that would come. I felt ashamed, dirty, disgusted, and unlovable as I would feel for the next twenty-two years. Yet, like so many other women, I blamed myself and stayed with Stan.

Fast forward a few years, when I started to question our relationship and began to wonder if this was the person I wanted for the rest of my life. Doubts began to fill my mind as he was pushing me to elope during our sophomore year of college. I told him I wasn't ready for marriage and that I needed a break. Tears streamed down his face as he told me that God had given him signs that we were destined to be together and that I was his soulmate. I tried to be strong. I took a break for a few weeks to clear my mind. There was a knock on my door late one evening. *Who could it be?* I thought, as I wasn't expecting company. I opened the door and found Stan on the other side.

He pushed his way into my apartment, dropped to the ground sobbing, holding my legs as he said, "I cannot live without you. I will kill myself if you don't take

me back. My life has no purpose without you in it."
Dread filled my heart and my stomach felt instantly
queasy. I thought my heart was going to explode at that
moment as thoughts raced through my mind: *I can't
live with myself if he dies. God brought us together, we are
soulmates, and no one will love you like this. You are not
worthy.*

"Okay," I said, "I love you and will take you back."

A carpet of red flags lined the altar as we got married just a year and a half later. My white wedding
dress and infectious smile hid the secrets of the past. I
remember telling myself the morning of my wedding
that nobody is perfect and that I should be happy that
I found someone, as no one would ever want someone
so dirty and ashamed. As I listened to my friend read,
"Love is patient, love is kind. It is not jealous, it is not
pompous, it is not inflated, it is not rude, it does not
seek its own interests, it is not quick-tempered, it does
not brood over injury, it does not rejoice over wrongdoing but rejoices with the truth," I prayed that these
words would ring true.

Within a year of exchanging our wedding vows, I
became pregnant with our first. Being a mother was
something I never imagined, given my medical history. At my initial appointment, the doctor stared at
me in disbelief and said it was a "miracle." A miracle
indeed, and maybe Stan was right that this was part
of God's plan. As soon as we got married, Stan said my
role was to be a wife and mother and to submit to him
as the "head of the household." My plans for graduate
school and international work were no longer a dream,

as I had to submit to "God's plan for us." I threw myself into pregnancy and my new identity as a mother.

I read books and went to La Leche League meetings and natural childbirth classes while pregnant to make sure I could be the best mother possible. Holding my daughter in my arms for the first time was indescribable and truly the first time I felt and received real love. My entire world changed at that moment. Being a mom became my mission. Two children later, our marriage was nonexistent. Pages of my journal were filled with sorrow and pleadings to God to take the pain away. Why was I not good enough? Would I ever be enough for him? Why didn't he love me? Would anyone love me?

My smile had faded, my belief in humanity was eroded, and I felt that I deserved this. I told myself to suck it up and stay strong because divorce was not an option. Every marriage has problems, right? It wasn't until my oldest daughter now in middle school kept asking me, "Why do you let Daddy be so mean to you? Why isn't he like other daddies who love mommies?" It was a wake-up call, like a cup of black coffee running through my veins.

Did I want her to marry someone like her dad? What kind of mother am I, allowing this kind of treatment to occur in front of the three souls I vowed to take care of and protect at any cost? I decided to see a therapist. Stan said, "Good, you are bipolar and crazy and overemotional, so maybe someone can finally get you help." The therapist helped me over the next few years to see that I was none of the things I had been told for so many years. I was worthy of love, respect, and partnership, and that something had to change. I got the courage to find a divorce attorney and filed for the first time. Shortly after I filed, Stan vowed to change, and again tears streamed down his face as he pledged his love for me. Like a flashback in time, he repeated that I was "his soulmate and couldn't live without me and the kids."

Deep down inside, I knew it was all a facade and a lie, but I still wanted my fairy-tale ending. I took him back on the condition that we would start marriage therapy and I could start to pursue a career. The promises were short-lived and the coercive control, and the psychological abuse, including verbal assaults, only intensified. Eleven months later, I filed for divorce for the second time and for good.

I somehow believed that the divorce would be fair, equitable, and just; after all, we had created three lives together. He said he would "honor me in the divorce, as I had sacrificed so much for his career and for the kids." Nothing could be further from the truth. I have been financially destroyed, annihilated in court, and told that I "poisoned my children against their father in an act of severe parental alienation."

Why did I not leave sooner? Why did I not try to keep the children safer from the abuse sooner? Somehow, I knew deep down inside, to the depths of my maternal core, that I could not protect them as well.

I knew that once I left Stan, our children would become the emotional punching bag. It was a decision no mother ever wanted or should make. I also knew that I was so broken inside from the abuse that I had little left to give. Most nights, I prayed that God would take me from this world. After I left, he charmed the kids like he had charmed me as a young teenager. The charm did not last long, as he found himself fired from his job and engaged in a fast and inappropriate relationship with a new mom while we were still separated. His actions and decisions created complete chaos, and the children suffered the most. His anger toward me blocked his ability to show love to his children.

Stan had been absent as a parent for most of their lives. Sure, he showed up to their school events and played with them outside occasionally, but he lacked the ability to connect on a deeper and emotional level with them, just as he had with me. He taught the children to disrespect me and that my role as a woman and mother was insignificant.

The last several years have been a living hell. One of my children has tried to take her life twice after suffering from emotional, psychological, and physical abuse at the hands of her father. In middle school, she got into a physical altercation with her father, which landed her in juvenile jail for assaulting him. The bruises left on her body were not enough for the police to charge him, and her father used this as an opportunity to say she attacked him instead. All she had done was react in self-defense by kicking him in the groin and yet she was the criminal, which landed her in jail at thirteen.

This event scared her other siblings and cemented their fear of their father. My oldest daughter responded by refusing visitation. This opened up a two-year modification suit and somehow ended with me losing custody of my youngest and all rights. Read that again. I lost custody of my children to an abuser. Stan claimed that I had engaged in severe parental alienation to explain the reasons why our older teenagers were refusing contact. Ignore the bruises of his daughter, his decision to press charges when she was a middle schooler, and overlook that he even engaged in an act of family violence with me during a custody exchange. None of that mattered. Stan was placed on six months of supervised visitation with our youngest following the altercation, and even that did not matter. The teenagers complied with the orders for reunification therapy and yet it wasn't enough. I was depicted as an alienator and an abuser. The last nine months since losing custody have been a blur. For nineteen years, my entire purpose for living has been a mother, and somehow, now I have been criminalized for that very thing that puts breath in my lungs and fills my soul with love.

The invisible bruises, scars, and wounds of emotional, financial, spiritual, verbal, and psychological abuse is criminal. The internal turmoil, distrust, and hatred of oneself that survivors frequently experience can paralyze your every thought and move. For close to two decades, these hidden scars created a wall around me and dictated how I could live and who I could interact with and even impacted my future dreams and hopes. Being under the control of an intimate partner was akin to living imprisoned in your own home.

Intimate partner violence crushed my self-esteem and the ability to discern my own intuition and trust in others.

But I want to leave you with this message: There is hope. I have broken the cycle with my oldest daughters. Leaving was the hardest thing I have ever done, but it was necessary to save my children. In my strength and anguish, they have learned to stand up for themselves and to never accept love disguised as abuse. My teenagers are now flourishing, as they have had no contact with their father for several years. I was able to protect two of my three and won't stop until my last one is safe.

NOTES

When someone asks, "How could you fall for a predator?" The answer is, it's actually quite easy. They have often been manipulating people since an early age. Plus, when they seem genuinely interested in your hopes, dreams, and deepest pain, it feels like that's exactly what the perfect guy is supposed to do (we are taught this). When you meet your "soulmate," as our culture demonstrates in movies and books, you tell them everything. The problem is that coercive controllers/narcissistic abusers are gathering all the information about your vulnerabilities like a detective at a crime scene. They store this information to use as a weapon against you.

In Sarah's case, Stan manipulated her by exploiting her desire for love and a stable family life. It was hard to resist. Being the empath she was, when he threatened suicide, she was compelled to get back together with him. Abusers target kind, compassionate people for a reason. They use those wonderful traits to trap their victims and usually secure their hand in marriage, before the mask really comes off and the abuse escalates. If she could go back in time, of course Sarah wishes she had not taken him back when they were dating. But she takes comfort in the fact that her daughters will hopefully make different choices. She is sharing her story to educate all the young women out there who may be trapped in the cycle of abuse. Her message? Get out now or, sadly, you could lose your kids later.

— Amy Polacko

A LIFE SENTENCE

Victoria's Story – United States

The unraveling of my once-happy marriage with Rex plunged me into a nightmare of unimaginable torment, marking the beginning of an indefinite and agonizing journey through the family court system. The turning point came when I discovered I was pregnant with our first child. Rex's demeanor shifted dramatically, signaling the onset of his escalating control, characterized by gaslighting, entitlement, insults, belittling, and patronizing behavior. He issued ultimatums, threatening divorce if I dared to defy his wishes—he wanted me to leave my career. Fearing the fracture of our family, I conceded, sacrificing my professional aspirations to become a stay-at-home mom. Little did I know this decision would only serve to strengthen Rex's coercive hold over me.

Nine years later, I would find out that not only was he an abuser in the home, but he was also a betrayer out of the home. For some reason, when the national news broke about many prominent individuals exposed as members of the Ashley Madison infidelity-focused dating website, I was curious. I sat in front of my computer screen, daring myself to see if Rex was on the list. I felt like I was suffocating. My heart raced as I scrolled through the list of names. And then, there it was, staring back at me with damning clarity: my husband's contact information, email address, and the unmistakable location of his downtown office. I couldn't believe it. My hands trembled as I absorbed the chilling truth revealed before me: He had created an account on this site nine years prior while I was working through contractions to bring our first child into the world. My husband was one of many people exposed by hackers of the Ashley Madison website: "Life is short. Have an affair." I felt an agonizing mix of emotions—shock, betrayal, disgust, and heartbreak.

Bringing our son into this world was one of the happiest days of my life, a day of joy and anticipation of our future as a family. The innocence of that moment, when I counted the months, weeks, and then minutes until I would hold our newborn in my arms, shattered irreparably against the cold reality of his deceit. The fact that while I was consumed with the miracle of new life, he was planning clandestine affairs with other married women, served as a turning point for me. I finally understood he was devoid of the capacity for genuine emotion or love, unlike most of humanity.

A mere month after surrendering my career dreams, Rex delivered a devastating blow— admitting to having unprotected sex with a sex worker he hired during an international hunting trip with his father and brother-in-law. The revelation was overwhelming with the possibility of exposing me and our unborn child to sexually transmitted diseases. I was expecting an apology or remorse but received nothing. The guilt and shame I felt knowing I couldn't shield my unborn child from potential harm were all-consuming. I turned to my OBGYN for medical reassurance, praying for negative results. Fortunately, we were spared, but the trauma remained. Trapped in a nightmarish reality with a twelve-month-old baby, five months pregnant with our second child, and the fresh wound of walking away from my career, I found myself ensnared in a web of Rex's coercive control, my vulnerability exploited at every turn.

For over a decade, I continued to work hard to keep us together—choosing our family over leaving a man I knew had no integrity. If only I knew the lengths he was willing to go, perhaps I would have stayed even longer. I poured my heart and soul into motherhood, cherishing every moment with our children. As their primary caregiver, I provided unwavering love, support, and guidance, attending all their school events, extracurricular activities, and being present for all major milestones. Despite the challenges we faced—infidelity, substance abuse, and mental health struggles that plagued Rex—I remained steadfast in my commitment to our family's well-being and never wavered in my dedication to creating a loving and stable environment for our children to thrive in.

As our children grew and flourished under my nurturing care, Rex's jealousy of our close and profound bond became increasingly evident. While I offered warmth and emotional connection, Rex remained rigid, controlling, and emotionally distant, unable to comprehend the depth of our mother-child relationship due to his own dysfunctional upbringing, marked by abuse at the hands of his parents. Rex's jealousy of my loving relationship with our children seemed to threaten his desire for absolute dominance and control, viewing us as possessions rather than individuals to be nurtured and deserving of respect.

His insidious efforts to undermine my relationship with our children—to turn them against me in his quest for control—became increasingly apparent. Now I know these efforts had started immediately and methodically. Rex's jealousy not only strained our family dynamic but also revealed the depths of his insecurities and his relentless pursuit of power and control. I now know this is par for the course for abusers. He wanted to hurt me and was willing to use the children to do so.

After thirteen years of marriage, I realized I could no longer keep up the facade. His tactics were overtly abusive, and the children were experiencing it as much as I was. We finally divorced, and I was awarded the exclusive right to choose the children's primary residence. Rex did not raise any issue regarding my mental health or fitness to properly parent our children. The dissolution of our marriage shattered any illusions of peace. I placed firm boundaries and distanced myself from him while the children spent about 50 percent of the time with him—typical in divorce—but something that should not be typical with an abuser. But, as I now

know, the systems do not acknowledge tactics by perpetrators.

I became hopeful when Rex remarried, thinking
he would move on from his obsession to control me.
However, it only intensified. I was left grappling with
the painful truth: Rex was never going to allow me
peace to rebuild a life outside of his control, and he
would use our children to silence and threaten me.
He was coercing the children into believing that my
duty was to meet his needs above the needs of anyone, including the children and myself. I knew this
was unhealthy and was determined to shield my children from the fallout. Little did I know the road ahead
would be fraught with injustice and heartache, as the
very system meant to uphold justice and safeguard
families would become my greatest adversary.

A little after one month of me securing primary
custody in the final decree of divorce, Rex weaponized
our children and the legal system against me through
a barrage of new lawsuits for modifications to regain
his control. It's almost like he purposefully agreed to
the original order only to torture me and try to pull the
rug out from underneath me and the children—like it
was a game. His relentless legal abuse and maneuvers,
spanning as of today eleven consecutive years, were
aimed at eroding my rights as a mother and severing
the bonds between me and my children while absolv-
ing himself of financial responsibilities.

With each passing day, Rex's grip tightened, suffocating any semblance of normalcy. His actions were
aggressive, malicious, and calculated, and our chil-

dren became unwitting casualties of his manipulation. On top of these new and disturbing legal tactics, the children began sharing stories of abuse, accompanied by physical evidence of their trauma.

As hearings loomed and accusations mounted, I found myself fighting not just for custody but for our very survival as a family. The family court system had become a weapon in Rex's hands. He was relentless and misrepresented my desire to protect my children—as my attempts to "alienate" him from the children. This culminated in a custody battle with Rex successfully thwarting a custody evaluation, any comprehensive investigation or evaluation of the children's outcries of abuse against him. I believed, I had to hope, that this would help our situation. He was refusing to collaborate while I had witnesses, including my children's teachers and pediatrician voicing concerns, validating my fears of their well-being under Rex's care.

Instead, Rex successfully created a narrative that deflected attention from his known abusive and problematic behaviors, blindly blaming me for his marred relationship with our children using self-serving rhetoric and generalizations, with no supporting evidence. I had no idea that this would lead to his successfully removing the children from my life completely—erasing me.

He was able to make unilateral decisions, in violation of court orders, which led to him hiring and consulting with a manager of a family reunification camp, who I will call Dave. This nonpracticing psychologist has a dubious reputation, as do "experts" at all reunification camps.

The supposed intent of reunification programs is to work toward repairing the relationship between the child and the supposed "estranged" parent, who is often also the abusive parent. Not all reunification programs are created equally, and not all of these programs physically remove children from their protective parents. However, reunification programs that are "camps" mandate expensive "treatment programs," with professionals claiming to specialize in "parental alienation." It is a life sentence for the children and the protective parent—the children are removed and literally ripped from the arms of the one parent they are attached to and feel safe with. It is a life sentence due to the trauma inflicted by the system. No one can give back this loss of time. No one can imagine the betrayal that the children feel. The end goal is to ensure the protective parent is punished—the systems complicit—with the goal that the children are never allowed to return to their protective parent. There are no words for the trauma experienced and the long road to healing that is preventable. Yes, it is a scam.

These camps purport to reunify children with a parent that they fear and want limited contact to and/ or refusing contact with. The intent is to force the children into "repair" therapy with a parent they may fear for a variety of reasons—including abuse to them or their other parent. I now know that Rex and Dave worked for months in advance to put in place a plan, unbeknownst to me, to remove my healthy children from me entirely and to force them into this camp. The payout of this plan provided a financial benefit around $500,000 to Rex's hired team. It was profit at the expense of our family—for a problem that didn't exist.

Dave, without ever speaking to me or the children, and with no active license, deemed our children to be "severely alienated" only after the children made outcries of abuse against their father, leading to a child protective services investigation. This paved the way for Rex to request the court eliminate me from the children's lives—a requirement of reunification camps. Ultimately, the camp profited, charging an estimated $10,000 per day, to consult and "run" the unregulated and experimental "stay away" hotel program with our children.

To date, I still don't know how the children "qualified" because Rex has refused to produce the intake or other related information. I feel nothing that the children or I did or didn't do was the catalyst for their being sent away, as it appears from emails produced that this was predetermined early on.

During the reunification camp hearing, injustice reigned, as all my witnesses and expert testimony were denied! Rex's were allowed free rein. The court's improper delegation of authority to Rex's paid expert further tilted the scales against me, culminating in the court's blind endorsement of the controversial family reunification camp. I was living in a nightmare.

I filed a motion, which alerted the court: "the Board disciplined Dave based on his unprofessional conduct in two different court proceedings ... Dave's conduct constituted an extreme departure from the standard of practice for a psychologist ... substantial evidence supports the trial court's finding that Dave was dishonest ... [in one case] Dave opined that a child [whom he had not evaluated] was severely alienated [and recommended and intervention program such as being requested here]." My children would be forced into Dave's care and placed in a hotel room for four days of "behavior modification intervention." This by a man who agreed to suspend his license in lieu of having it revoked, for forcing children into "reunification camp."

My witnesses and experts would have given valuable information about me; the dangers of the unregulated and controversial family reunification therapies, including reunification camps; and critical information about the children's well-being, including the risks of being separated from their mother. Justice demands the court should have allowed evidence and testimony from both parties, not just Rex, for such a serious decision as an effective termination of my parental rights by eliminating all contact and communication between me and the children indefinitely. I was prohibited from a fair hearing and from presenting any sort of defense about my actual behaviors with the children and their outcries.

My former counsel expressed concern, saying, "This essentially is a shadow court deciding and doing everything outside of this court, and we know nothing about it." Rex paid thousands of dollars for this family reunification camp expert, who explained to the court that the camp requires a minimum ninety-day no-contact order because "In the early days, they didn't have the ninety-day exclusionary period, and they found that children relapsed the sooner that the favored parent was reintroduced and, so . . . they made the ninety-day [no-contact order] and have found that that is a sufficient period of time."

I expressed my fears and concerns that, through my own research, I understood that these camps are very problematic and that they have been known to switch custody from the preferred parent to the parent the children claim is abusive. The experimental and unregulated four-day deprogramming of the children in a hotel and their ninety-day minimum of no contact to the safe and preferred parent is known to be a distraction. It is used to convince courts to order the no contact, under the guise that it is "short-term" and temporary.

I conveyed my concern about the intentionally vague aftercare role of this camp, which is used as the vehicle to keep children separated from their favored parent for years by design, because there is no defined way to successfully complete. I knew somewhere at my core that this would be a life sentence.

Reunification camps are never just ninety days and often isolate the child by preventing any contact or communication with their safe and preferred parent until the child turns eighteen or emancipates, which, in our case, was six and eight years away. The court was alerted about concerns of trauma and harm the children may suffer. I submitted about eight affidavits from other children who aged out and shared their horror stories from being forced to participate in the family reunification camp and the extreme trauma and long-term effects from being separated from their safe and preferred parent. The court said: "I'm not aware of anyone that's going to keep the children from their mother for two years."

My biggest fear has become my very painful reality. And exactly what experts warned me: These "alienation" programs and camps operate under the guise of preserving the relationship between the parents and children and do the exact opposite.

When I was the primary parent, my children had both parents in their lives. The children were not estranged from Rex. They did not reject their father; they wanted a better relationship with him. Rex wanted obedience and control and ultimately to hurt me in an unimaginable way. His strategy worked. He and his team cut off all access between me and the children and kept us in a situation where we have no way of knowing when we will see each other again.

The court decided that Rex's problematic relationship with the children may be fixed under a "temporary order" by an immediate change in custody. They were taken to an undisclosed hotel where Dave and his team implemented their "intervention"—their intense and experimental programming. The children were forcibly placed under the exclusive care of their father, restricted to a relationship solely with him. The children were traumatized by not being allowed to say goodbye to their mother, grandmother, pets, or home. They were isolated from anyone in their past who they love and trust. They were enrolled in a new school, had their doctors changed, and were prevented from receiving individual counseling or trauma care. An indefinite forced mother-child separation and trauma was dictated as the cure while mandating expensive and unregulated "treatment" protocols.

The children were forced into this camp because Rex alleged parental alienation. Yet this was never a finding in our case. The children were deprived of knowing or having access to their mother during the most crucial years of their lives—a cruel and senseless separation spanning thus far over six long and agonizing years.

Recently, professionals who were involved in the case were subpoenaed, and I was able to see records. No parent should have to read these documents. They detail what my children had endured since Rex was allowed exclusive control to make mental health and medical decisions without my input. My heart shattered into a million irreparable pieces. No healthy parent would ever subject their child into forced reunification, whether through therapy or another intervention, or—the most heinous— a reunification camp. These "interventions" are intended to change a child's beliefs, a brainwashing that is none other than coercive and controlling of the child and subjecting them to trauma unimaginable.

The pain of discovering the depths of their suffering, from the insidious behavior modification to the manipulation of their memories, left me utterly devastated, realizing the agony they endured without my knowledge or ability to protect them. The anguish of knowing they were forced to doubt their own reality, robbed of their mother, grandmother, childhoods, their identity, robbed of the love and memories we once shared, fills me with an indescribable sorrow that no words could ever express. This heart-wrenching reality underscores the devastating psychological impact caused by their father and the complicit court system.

The children have endured a harrowing ordeal, subjected to coercion, threats, and manipulative tactics that included behavior modification, exposure to videos intended to distort their perceptions of reality, and coerced engagement in lessons aimed at implanting false memories. They were deceived into believing the reunification camp wielded the power to enforce a "moratorium," effectively erasing their past and any memories of me from their lives. Records revealed my son's heartbreaking belief that he is not allowed to remember the past, and all his memories before this reunification camp were wiped away. Additionally, my daughter, denied access to therapy to cope with the loss of our relationship, resorted to convincing herself that I was dead to ease her pain. That was another sad fact I found by reading through the subpoenaed documents. This fabricated moratorium also served as a tool to silence them from discussing any abuse from their father, further compounding their suffering, and depriving them of their voices and truths.

I was intentionally excluded from the intense four-day treatment. Despite the children's cooperation, the promised reunion after ninety days never materialized, as the rules were continually changed, prolonging their isolation from me for almost six years at the request of their father. Rex deprived the children of any form of contact or communication with me—no calls, texts, Zoom sessions, letters, birthday cards, or gifts—effectively cutting them off from my presence and love for all of middle school and high school.

The children cooperated and did everything asked of them to prove their "readiness" to improve their relationship with Rex to his satisfaction, with the hopes to earn back their right to have their mother in their life. I also faithfully adhered to court orders. I diligently completed all set forth tasks before the ninety days were up. Yet, as the promised reunion loomed, I faced yet another disappointment. The aftercare professional, ordered to be an "educator" and follow the reunification camp "playbook," abruptly shifted course after I completed all known tasks and unilaterally decided that she would be veering away from the protocol and would now impose her own undefined agenda.

Despite investing around $10,000 and enduring ten sessions, the aftercare process proved to be coercive and abusive, with the aftercare professional showing no intention of facilitating a reunion with my children within the promised ninety days, if ever. I was pressured to retract any abuse allegations and shoulder full responsibility for the strained relationship between my children and their father, under the implicit threat that I would never see my children again unless I admitted to what they wanted. Over six years of relentless manipulation followed, with the aftercare professional continually altering the rules, adding sessions, and demanding more money, all while evading accountability by claiming there was no set curriculum. In her testimony, she stated, "I've tried my best to explain that it is a process and that I'm not able to give a definitive answer ... There is no set curriculum."

The aftercare professional's refusal to define her process, and then her refusal to remove herself to allow me to work with a neutral person, caused me severe agony, prolonging the children's separation from me and leaving me in helplessness and despair.

My son is now seventeen and my daughter is sixteen. Under "temporary orders," I have not been allowed contact or communication with my children for almost six years after Rex successfully convinced the court to order our children to attend a reunification camp. This is despite the fact that no party has ever alleged—and the court has never found—that I am unfit or a danger to our children. I remain a joint managing conservator, confirming that I am not a danger to the children's physical or psychological well-being.

The unjust temporary orders and no-contact order continue, despite the significant amount of work I've done to show my sincerity and willingness to follow court orders to be reunited with my children. And despite the children's extreme desire to see me, six years later, there is still no custody evaluation, no forensic evaluation of the children, no diagnosis, no treatment plan, no timeline, no concrete steps, or deadline to reunite me with the children I love and miss dearly and who desperately need me in their lives.

The lack of concrete steps towards reunification and the crazy-making circular reasoning has left me trapped in this helpless maze of inescapability, where no matter how much I did to be reunited with my children, it was never enough for me to earn back my constitutional right to know, love, and raise my children. I am condemned to an interminable limbo of shattered hopes and unfilled promises.

NOTES

Victoria hasn't had contact with her children for over six years. Victoria expressed concern for her children—and her children were expressing concern to her. Victoria was not abusive. Like other mothers in this book, Victoria is a loving protective mother devoted to her children. Her crime? Divorcing a coercive controller/narcissistic abuser who co-opted the term alienation.

When coercive controllers/narcissistic abusers are emboldened, weaponizing the children and seeking more custody or full custody is the ideal strategy for harming the protective parent. For all intents and purposes, the court system rolls out the red carpet to exert further coercion and control—and the results are devastating.

Victoria's ex used the pseudoscience parental alienation syndrome against her. The syndrome, created by Richard Gardner (1985) without valid research, states that children often lie about abuse and mothers who claim that their children are abused are "alienating" fathers. This alleged syndrome was determined to arise primarily in the context of child custody disputes and involves a child's "unjustified estrangement" from a parent with Gardner who had extremely harmful pro-child sexual abuse beliefs, discussed in depth in his work, such as "pedophilia also serves procreative purposes" (1987).

Who is deciding if the child has unjustified estrangement from a parent? Lawyers and judges. What if the parent was abusive, as was the case with Victoria's ex? It doesn't matter. What if a mother knows full well that her children are not safe with the abusive ex? And what if the children express fear? The dark underbelly of family court would have us believe that a history of abuse within the parental subsystem is not relevant.

Court professionals are not trauma trained nor trained on the character traits of abusers and how these abusers further exert coercive control within the systems intended to protect adult and child victims. We have a multitude of research describing the character traits of these abusers. Coercive controllers/narcissistic abusers, due to their character traits are wholeheartedly invested in revenge, with the children serving as the ultimate retaliation weapon. As Dr. Evan Stark states, children are secondary victims, not because they are irrelevant, but because they are the most efficient access to harming the protective parent (2023).

Along with other major organizations (listed in our Call to Action at the end of the book), including the American Medical Association, The United Nations Human Rights Council Special Report (April 2023) recommended that the use of parental alienation and reunification camps be prohibited.

Forcing children into repair therapy or to a reunification program with someone they feel unsafe with, oftentimes the abusive parent, is coercive control of the children. The alienation industry profits on the backs of protective parents and their children. Clinicians know, and any child development specialist recognizes, that the attachment that a child has with a parent or a caretaker should not be severed. Forcing children into treatment with someone they feel "unsafe" with simply to punish a protective parent is extremely harmful to the psychological well-being of the developing brain. Secure attachment is a primal need. In these cases, children are ripped from the arms of the one parent they feel securely attached to. It's a retraumatization of children already traumatized by the perpetrators' abusive tactics within the parental subsystem. It's compound child abuse—by the coercive controller/narcissistic abuser—and by the systems. It's unconscionable.

Mandating access with an abuser, or, in this case (and so many others), robbing a mother entirely of her children and the children of their mother, is not a deviation from the norm, but tragically is the norm of family court. The stage is set, and the court becomes the stage for the characterologically disordered individual who is able to engage others in the horror show.

Ethical codes of practice include "Do no harm." All child welfare professionals, including clinicians, attorneys, custody evaluators, and forensic evaluators, must adhere to the ethical codes of practice, yet are making decisions that forcibly remove children from the one parent to whom the children feel a strong attachment. Reunification camps remove the ability for children to have autonomy in their own life and compound this trauma. It is clear that coercive control tactics, indoctrination, and reprogramming are used to alter the internal belief system of the children. This does not adhere to ethical codes of practice.

Repair and reunification therapies, of any kind, epitomize the exertion of coercive control on our children. As is evident, reunification camps are the worst-case scenario, giving a child a life sentence with their abuser and, as if there is a comparison, a life sentence of attempting to heal from a trauma that should have never occurred. Victoria's children's lives would have been so different had the courts protected them from the coercive controller/narcissistic abuser. Professionals performing and enforcing these therapies must be held accountable. They are inflicting one of the greatest travesties of our generation.

— Dr. C

WHO WAS PROTECTING KAYDEN?

Testimony of Kathryn Sherlock, mother of Kayden Mancuso, before the Pennsylvania General Assembly, opposing a House bill addressing child custody in 2019.

"We know there was a substantial history between the mother and father, an ongoing custody dispute. I don't know all the details yet, but we do know it was a very contentious relationship," Captain John Ryan, head of homicide in Philadelphia, stated in his interview with ABC News not even an hour after my daughter, Kayden Mancuso, was found dead.

The story hit breaking news on every channel, heard around the country, even internationally. Cameras arrived at my house not even hours later and the news spread like wildfire. And in almost every publication, the story reported always included "the custody dispute" and "the brutal custody battle." The headlines read "Child Killed Amongst Custody Dispute" and "Father Murders Daughter Amidst Custody Battle." No one ever discussed the actual issues at hand, that despite his violent past and his threats, he was still awarded parenting time with a little child by the courts—that he was mentally unstable, suicidal, violent, abusive, etc. —they just mention the "custody dispute."

In the initial news report, you can see them in the background bringing my daughter out in the body bag my father looks on in utter despair; he insisted on staying on scene until they took her out, making sure she was handled properly; you can see my husband collapsed on the ground on the other side of the house hysterical. You can see white sheets, crime scene investigators, the medical examiner van, and so on. The brutal murder of a seven-year-old child, like it was a scene out of a movie, but it wasn't a movie—it was my new reality.

My beautiful, full of life, amazing, gorgeous, talented, smart, spunky best friend and all-around amazing daughter was brutally beaten to death by her father. He beat her over and over again in the head with a thirty-five-pound dumbbell, not murdered with a gun as most kids are, but a dumbbell. She was found by the door with her shoes on, found by my father and husband the morning after she should have been returned home per our custody court order. She was found by the door, because she was trying to get away from the one person who should have cared for her, her own father.

I had to tell her at one point during all we endured that if she ever felt scared around her dad to run, I needed her to run and to find an adult and have them call me or the police. Run and run fast, because I knew what he was capable of. But despite my pleas, my worst nightmare came true, she was found by the door, beaten to death. He beat her and beat her and didn't stop until she couldn't fight anymore, but she did fight for her little life. After he beat her till he thought she was dead enough for him, he flipped her over, tied a Wawa plastic bag around her head, and secured it with an iPhone charger cord, to make sure she wouldn't survive. He then washed his hands and took his time to write a two-page letter, as his daughter's lifeless body lay on the floor, and threw it on her dead body. The note stated: "You all get what you deserve." No matter what I told them about how dangerous he was, the courts wouldn't believe me, and they decided this person should have unsupervised parenting time with my daughter because he was her dad and it was his "parental right."

He then went upstairs, made sure his previously written suicide note was in sight, tied a belt around his neck tied it to the door, anticipating passing out from the nitrous, which would make his body hang itself, took whip (the nitrous oxide), and killed himself. This happened over his custodial weekend in August after the judge awarded them to him in May of 2018, denying my request for supervised visits. This happened eighteen months after court proceedings started and to what the media, and all the decision-makers, including the judge himself, the court system, and the police involved—coined "the contentious custody battle." I was the defendant in the case; court was used as a way to intimidate and control, bankrupt, and punish me.

We spent eighteen months in actual custody litigation, and many years before we made a court appearance we had privately hired lawyers attempting to handle the "dispute" ourselves outside of court. I trusted the people I hired to help me, I had faith in a system—the justice system—I had no idea about. And they all failed, they failed my daughter, and she lost her beautiful life due to it. I was accused of "parental alienation" early on. I remember receiving a letter early on from his attorney, claiming that I was "alienating"—not protecting—Kayden, that I was keeping her from him on purpose to be spiteful, because I was a nasty rotten spiteful person (by "keeping her from him" he meant not willingly agreeing to a 50-50 custody agreement). That is how it all started.

In the early years, he would show up when he wanted, when he couldn't be bothered with actual parenting duties, and he took her when he felt like it and did what he wanted. If I said no I was harassed all day. If he couldn't get to me he would go to my family, his family, whoever he felt was in his path. He never stopped, for years. He wanted his way and no one was going to tell him no. Not a lawyer, court, judge, nor police. He googled the term of this bogus "alienation" theory and used it as a tactic in court to distract from what the real issues were, Kayden's safety and well-being, that I brought up in court. I voiced my concerns with the judge over and over again. I begged them to listen to me. I begged everyone to listen to what I was saying and to listen to what Kayden was saying. I was trying to get just one person to help me, pleading with my own attorney. I called everyone I thought I could, CPS, police, the courts, the evaluators, the psychiatrist, people at her school, family members, friends, everyone. Trying to get someone to listen to me.

I knew what he was capable of. I lived it. "Well, he's not physically harming her, nothing we can do." It fell on deaf ears. Not agreeing to what he wanted made me "difficult" in the view of the courts. Statements released by the AOPC (Administrative Office of Pennsylvania Courts) said that we both had "questionable" behavior. I was and am *still* blamed for his brutal murder of my daughter, called every name in the book from people all over the world, telling me things like "Sleep in the bed you made." After Jeff murdered Kayden, the judge who had awarded him parenting time released a statement stating: "Let this toxic relationship and contentiousness be a teachable moment to all of you." A teachable moment? My child is gone, and the judge cannot even acknowledge his decision to award the murderer access to my child led to her death.

I have heard from people from all over the world, mostly moms, each one begging me to help them with their own custody issues, asking for advice, sharing stories so similar to what I went through in court, each one saying, "I don't want my child to be the next Kayden." Tough words to hear. Sadly I have no advice to give them, what I did in court didn't work for me. I buried a beautiful seven-year-old after spending thousands and thousands of dollars in a system I had faith in, that I thought would protect her, that should have protected her. No parent should have to bury her children, especially where it could have so easily been prevented.

Parental rights supersede children's rights in our family courts, and *this is backwards*. Some people are evil and shouldn't have kids or be around kids or even humans. He wouldn't have been able to adopt and have a dog because of his violent history, but humans were fine according to family law. Kayden's father's "parental rights" superseded her right to live. Every judge, candidate, lawyer, or court personnel I have talked to all say the same thing: that the best interest of the child comes first. But it doesn't. In practice, it doesn't. Passing a 50-50 presumption custody bill as that of HB1397 being introduced into the House would be detrimental to the safety of kids.

It would make it worse than it already is. Kids' safety and *actual* best interest should be the number one priority in all custody cases. Number one priority. The end. There shouldn't even be a discussion about it—it should be the norm. Again it's not. Protective parents are viewed as "alienators." The courts take this bogus theory (written by a dead pedophile apologist, Richard Gardner), which abusers use to challenge real abuse claims or safety risks for the child, over anything else. Over the child's best interest. You hear the word "*alienation*" (like Jeff claimed against me, her mom trying to protect her) and all of a sudden all other information or testimony, witnesses, and experts and all of that is dismissed or ignored by the courts. Claiming "alienation" works for dangerous parents. All the real evidence gets brushed over then and kids get handed over to abusive parents on silver platters. "Alienation" claims are used against protective parents, and the protectors are then punished and threatened by the courts if they keep trying to get their kids to safety. Punished, gagged, safe parent's rights are reduced or even terminated, some safe parents are thrown in jail for "civil" matters—trying to protect their kids from dangerous abuse which protectors know is happening but courts ignore or disbelieve.

I don't deny that divorcing or separating parents sometimes say bad things about the other. It occurs, but the weight that it holds in family court in these custody cases is absurd and detrimental. By passing a bill like HB1397, it would only aid in making family court that much more dangerous to our kids and their safety. Kids are *not* property. They have the right under our Constitution to be protected like any other human. Kids' rights are human rights.

NOTES

Kathryn Sherlock has honored her daughter Kayden's memory by working tirelessly to campaign for family court reform and the protection of children. She and Danielle Pollack, policy manager at the National Family Violence Law Center at George Washington University, saw their efforts come to fruition on March 16, 2022, at the White House. That's when President Biden signed the reauthorization of the Violence Against Women's Act (VAWA), which included the *Keeping Children Safe From Family Violence Act*, known as *Kayden's Law*. This legislation limits the power of abusers to weaponize our family court system against a protective parent and receive custody of children. It must, however, be passed in each state and that process has begun.

Danielle Pollack shared this legislative update on *Kayden's Law* at the time of our printing:

"It is encouraging to see our long-term strategic policy work coming to fruition as states move to adopt the child safety provisions of the federal *Keeping Children Safe From Family Violence Act*, also known as '*Kayden's Law*,' which is named after a little girl in Pennsylvania who was preventably murdered by her abusive father after family court granted him unsupervised parenting time. Colorado was the first state to adopt the four key interdependent elements of *Kayden's Law* since federal enactment in 2022, and this legislative session [2024] Utah followed suit with '*Om's Law*,' which draws on those same provisions and is named after Om Moses Gandhi. Om, like Kayden and Piqui and many other children, was also preventably abused and killed by his dangerous father following a court order, despite ample abuse evidence being put forward during litigation by his protective mom.

"Other states that have adopted the *Kayden's Law* provisions, at least in part, include Tennessee ('*Abrial's Law*'), California ('*Piqui's Law*'), Maryland, Arizona, and Pennsylvania. Several other states have bills introduced and are working on advancing those key provisions, which 1) require family courts to consider all past evidence of family violence when making child custody decisions,

2) mandate judicial and court personnel training in eight subjects on family violence, 3) limit expert evidence on abuse to only those appropriately qualified, and 4) limit courts from ordering "reunification treatments/camps," which are unsafe for children and cut them off from their safe parent."

— Amy Polacko

EPILOGUE

By Tina Swithin, founder of One Mom's Battle

I remember that Saturday—an eerily quiet, warm evening in August 2009—like it was yesterday.

I stood in a dark, musty room at my local women's shelter with my laptop perched precariously on the windowsill. It wasn't that this was a comfortable surface to draft my family court documents, but it was the only place I could find to connect to neighboring Wi-Fi. In a race with time—and a fight for my family—I stood at the windowsill and scrolled through the court website, desperately studying various forms and procedures.

How has this become my life? I wondered.

Standing alone in a dimly lit shelter room, I felt the crushing weight of the present moment. The future of my little girls, and the unknowns that awaited us, rested squarely on my shoulders. Over a decade later, the thoughts and feelings from this moment are imprinted into my mind, body, and soul. These embodied memories reflect the intensity of survivors' trauma, regardless of how much time has passed.

All it takes is a thought, smell, or sound, and we are instantly teleported back to that place in time: for me, a lonely windowsill. This is a reality that only a survivor can truly understand.

That August, in between drafting my court declaration and attempting to make sense of the legal process, I reflected on what brought me to that shelter room. The year leading up to that month was explosive in every category: financial, familial, professional, personal. Toward the end of 2008, I discovered that my soon-to-be ex-husband was a con artist, leaving our family in over one million dollars of debt. The fallout was catastrophic and involved the loss of my home, my beloved business, and my marriage. My car was slated for repossession and I was forced to file bankruptcy, leaving only $178 to my name.

Everything was gone, yet I recognized our finances as merely material possessions—especially when compared to my two young daughters, whose immediate safety mattered to me above all else. But financial status fueled my ex-husband's ego and identity. When we lost our security, my world became a dark and scary place. I watched him spiral into a dark abyss—and as he hit rock bottom, I feared for my life and the lives of my daughters.

On that fateful Saturday in August, I awoke to three terrifying voicemails from my husband. Without any further deliberation, I placed my pajama-clad little girls in the backseat of my car and sought safety at the local women's shelter. As with other memories of this time, I remember and feel this moment in my body:

by far the rawest, most humbling experience of my life. Uncertainty and chaos followed us to the shelter and well beyond, but I felt a sense of empowerment as I chose to stand in my truth; and eventually, I stood alongside other survivors as they held fast to their own. I felt confident in my decision to leave my ex-husband, reinforced by one of the most common societal messages aimed at victims of domestic abuse: be brave and leave.

With this message in mind, and coupled with encouragement from my marriage therapist, I thought I had cleared the biggest hurdle by freeing myself—and, in turn, my daughters—from a toxic and abusive relationship. I believed the worst was behind us, and I anticipated that everything to follow was simply logistical in nature. I knew that my role was to tell the truth about what we had endured, and I assumed that the professionals in the family court system would prioritize the safety and best interests of our children.

Just days after moving into the women's shelter, I walked through the doors of the family court for the very first time. Unable to afford legal representation, I acted as my own attorney, which didn't feel intimidating: after all, I was the expert in my case and in my life. In my naivete, I operated under the notion that the system existed to protect me and my children. In my hands, I gripped my truth in the form of court declarations and evidence of my ex-husband's instability and terrifying messages. I was confident that the transcripts of my husband's threatening voicemails and my decision to flee to the women's shelter would solidify the judge's decision in my favor.

Yet after spending only a few minutes reviewing our paperwork, the judge looked up and said: "If this is the way the two of you are going to start your divorce proceedings, you are both crazy." In seconds, the floor beneath my feet started to feel shaky and unstable: just as uncertain as my future. I questioned whether I heard him correctly. The room began to spin as I heard the judge's final ruling: unsupervised parenting time starting the following weekend. I felt waves of nausea take over my body.

I stood in this moment as my own advocate, wholly unprepared for the reality of the family court system—and I was just as stunned by my ex-husband's decision to pursue custody of our children. I reflected on the biggest source of contention during our marriage: his ongoing refusal to help with the children or connect with them in any way. As I read my ex-husband's court declarations, I was haunted by memories of our four-year-old daughter, who hid whenever he came home from work because of his unpredictable temper. I quickly realized that his legal pursuit of the children had nothing to do with his love for them and everything to do with his need to maintain power and control over me. The family court system became his new platform of manipulation, and the post-separation abuse was far more painful than the abuse I endured during our marriage.

I still remember the day I heard him utter the word *alienation*, lifted straight from The Abuser's Playbook.

"She is alienating our children from me," he said. I remember being confused and researching the term to fully understand his accusation. I wondered if I was reading the wrong information. There's no way he could accuse me of turning the children against him, I thought. His volatile temperament and abusive behavior had caused the children to fear him; but suddenly, the court proceedings asked me to assume ownership for his relationship with our daughters.

Fortuitously enough, this accusation unfolded in 2010 before the "alienation industry," also known as reunification profiteers, established a lucrative stronghold in the family court system. While my ex-husband's accusation required a strong defense, I managed to successfully disprove his assertion; but in our present-day family court system, I doubt I would have fared as well as I did then.

My story is not unique. In fact, it is the story of many survivors around the world. From start to finish, my family court nightmare spanned ten years with some legal loose ends, totaling fourteen years of negotiations, advocacy, and continual returns to the trauma that brought me here, transcribing my story in an epilogue.

Over those fourteen years, I represented myself in almost sixty court hearings, two separate trials, the appointment of minor's counsel, and two child custody evaluations. I navigated over a dozen interactions with law enforcement and multiple reports to child protective services, which deemed my ex-husband a "moderate risk" but did nothing to protect my children. There was also a criminal trial that spanned five years and threatened to destroy me.

As I sit here at my desk all these years later, it's difficult to accept that my daughters and I are considered "lucky" simply because I finally succeeded in terminating my ex-husband's parental rights. After hearing our story in full, the label "lucky" speaks volumes about the state of our family court system. While termination of parental rights does bring a sense of peace, my brain has yet to accept the fact that we are legally safe from our abuser. I have been diagnosed with complex post-traumatic stress disorder and it has taken a significant toll on my health. Many are shocked to know that, in hindsight, I am grateful that I could not afford legal counsel.

Acting as my own attorney was the most difficult but bravest thing I've ever done, and I do not believe I would have had such a successful outcome if I had financial resources and legal representation. Even "good" attorneys become part of the growing industry built around family court, where human lives are conveniently reduced to case numbers and business transactions. Because I began this journey at the lower end of the financial scale, I was never targeted by unscrupulous professionals who turn childhood trauma into revenue streams. By prioritizing parental rights over the safety of children, these individuals support a nefarious industry through which children are "reunified" with abusive parents. These so-called professionals are financially incentivized to push "pro-contact at all costs": a strategy that pads their wallets but consistently overrides the best interests of children.

It would be easy to stay in a place of anger and resentment toward the system and individuals who failed me and my daughters. I've had my moments over the years, but I have chosen to funnel my fury into advocacy efforts: through legislative change, awareness campaigns, and the provision of personalized support and resources to those who follow in my footsteps. In many ways, I have become the person I desperately needed during the darkest parts of my journey. Yet even when surrounded by love and support, many survivors continue to grapple with traumatic memories and feelings of isolation. While their supporters may be well-intentioned, they can't truly understand what it's like unless they have directly experienced the horrors of the family court system. Although we wish our experiences upon no one, there are many of us who "get it" because we've lived it—and together, we will be the change and support we so desperately need.

If you feel framed or relate to any portion of this book, this is your official call to action. We will start seeing change when our neighbors, friends, loved ones, community members, and elected officials link arms with us and stand in our collective truth, announcing: "No more." Together, with and for other survivors, we've created the community we need to enact this change and ignite our truths. Now it's time for our community to mobilize and get involved at every level of the cause: whether we generate awareness through word-of-mouth, legislative change, writing our stories, or bringing them under the media spotlight. What is done in the darkness will always come to light—and we vow to turn the lights on to the brightest setting.

Please know that you are not alone. We see you, and we see your light even if it feels dim in this moment; we hear you, and we stand with you always.

CALL TO ACTION

Often, those who have experienced family court injustice—or those who learn about what can happen there—ask, "What can I do?" It's simple.

Get involved on your local or state/province/region level, where laws to protect adult and child victims are created. Reform begins with a small group of dedicated advocates. Advocates also ensure that these laws are implemented as intended. Grassroots efforts work! Here's a primer on what every person who wants to join this cause needs to know.

IMPORTANT POLICY INITIATIVES YOU CAN GET BEHIND

The Basics of Child Safety Legislation

T he impetus of child safety legislation is in direct response to the number of children who are murdered during custodial time with an abusive parent. Prior to 2022, there was no single piece of legislation in the United States that ensured that child safety was the number one factor in determining child custody.

Concerns by protective parents about the safety of their children have historically been dismissed or entirely ignored. Protective parents know that failure to follow through with court orders may be seen as an obstruction of these orders. It's a tightrope no protective parent should be forced to walk.

Perpetrators know what matters most to the protective parent—the physical and psychological safety of the children. The coercive controller/narcissistic abusers need to exert power and control. Coercive control over the adult (targeted) victim, often is limitless, using systems to further inflict harm and wielding family court to gain more custodial time as retaliation. The intent is to harm the adult victim. Children become the casualties of this "revenge tactic." Sadly, all too often filicide (the murder of children) is the end result. In case after case, protective parents beg court professionals to heed their warnings about their children being unsafe with an abusive parent, their pleas falling on deaf ears.

As the stories in this book indicate, it is imperative that court professionals understand the pathology of perpetrators and also their responsibility in protecting victims, adults, and children from these perpetrators. The United States and other countries are woefully behind implementing this mandatory education.

STATUS IN VARIOUS COUNTRIES REGARDING CHILD SAFETY LEGISLATION

United States: *VAWA with Kayden's Law*

In October 2022, the Violence Against Women's Act (VAWA) was reauthorized with Kayden's Law—The Keeping Children Safe from Family Violence Act. As Kathryn Sherlock's story indicates, as of this writing, there are now five states in the United States that have passed Kayden's Law. Florida's Greyson's Law and other states have pushed for their own version of child safety legislation—like New York where protective mother Jacqueline Franchetti has been advocating for Kyra's Law. These efforts are almost entirely grassroots, galvanized by protective mothers who are demanding accountability for family court professionals. All these laws are named in honor of a child who has been murdered by a divorcing/separating parent. The Center for Judicial Excellence, a national nonprofit, reports the number of children murdered by a separated, divorced or court-involved parent. As of this writing, more than 989 children have died in these cases since the center started tracking data in 2008.

The intent of Kayden's Law is to ensure that judges and court professionals receive adequate training to understand abuse, and their grave responsibility in protecting children from perpetrators.

Kayden's Law: The Keeping Children Safe from Family Violence Act:

1. Restricts expert testimony to only those who are appropriately qualified to provide it.

2. Limits the use of reunification camps and therapies, which cannot be proven to be safe and effective.

3. Provides evidence-based ongoing training to judges and court personnel on family violence subject matter.

4. States that courts must consider evidence of past sexual or physical abuse, including protection orders, arrests, and convictions for domestic violence, sexual violence, or child abuse of the accused parent.

Canada: *Keira's Law*

In May 2023, Canada passed Keira's Law, amending the Judges Act to include continuing education for judges on intimate partner violence (IPV) and coercive control. When courts make decisions about a child, these decisions must be guided by only the best interests of the child. What's new as of March 1, 2021, is a list of specific factors that the court and spouses can consider when deciding what's in a child's best interests. The court must give priority to the child's physical, emotional, and psychological safety, security, and well-being when considering these factors:

1. The child's views and preferences

2. Any court action or order relevant to the child's safety and well-being

3. Any family violence

THE BASICS OF EQUAL SHARED PARENTING RESPONSIBILITY LEGISLATION

It is inaccurate to presume that equal time-sharing responsibility is always in the best interest of children. It is common for one parent to fulfill the role of the primary caregiver to the children. Inevitably, the children are more attached to this parent. In determining custody, it is ideal that children spend most of their time with the parent who has been primarily engaged in their care. In some cases, shared parenting may be in the best interest of the children; however, to make this a presumption without assessing for coercive control within the parental subsystem is placing both adult and child victims of abuse at risk. Even when laws include exemptions for family violence, presumptions undercut consideration of these abuse allegations.

STATUS IN VARIOUS COUNTRIES REGARDING EQUAL SHARED PARENTING RESPONSIBILITY LEGISLATION

United States: *50-50 Presumption for Shared Custody*

Some states are implementing an "equal shared parental responsibility" policy, presuming that 50-50 custody is in the best interest of the child! This legislation has passed in six states, and is pending in many other states. It must be stopped. Find out if your state has enacted this legislation or reach out to advocates attempting to prevent its passage.

Australia: *The Family Law Amendment Act*

In October 2023, the Australian Parliament passed the Family Law Amendment Act and the Family Law Amendment (Information Sharing) Act. These represent major legal changes about how Australian courts make parenting decisions in the best interests of a child. The laws took effect in May 2024 and repealed a legal presumption introduced in 2006 stating it was in the best interest of children for parents to have "equal shared parental responsibility." Fathers' rights groups pushed for this equal custody law but, in cases where there was domestic abuse, children were put in danger.

BASICS OF PARENTAL ALIENATION SYNDROME

At its inception, "parental alienation syndrome" (PAS) was created by Richard Gardner, who had extremely harmful, pro–child sexual abuse beliefs, discussed in depth in his work, such as "pedophilia also serves procreative purposes" (Gardner 1992, 24). The syndrome embodies the notion that when a child (or the primary parent) resists contact with the noncustodial parent without "legitimate" reason, the preferred parent is "alienating" the child due to her own anger, hostility, or pathology (Zaccour 2018). It has since been affirmed to be a pseudoscience founded upon "junk science" (Thomas and Richardson 2015, 1). PAS is the only diagnosis made by lawyers and judges without any regard for the underlying power dynamics in the parental subsystem—where coercive control lives and breathes.

Experts agree that the use of parental alienation is significantly gendered. It is a powerful tool used by abusive fathers with great success to wield coercive control over the targeted victim when she has expressed concerns about the safety of her children, thereby harming the children in these family systems (Dalgarno et al. 2023).

In April of 2023, the United Nations Human Rights Council Special Rapporteur (expert on human rights), Reem Alsalem, recommended that the use of parental alienation and reunification camps be prohibited. In 2020, the World Health Organization removed parental alienation from the International Classification of Diseases (ICD-11).

Parental alienation syndrome has been dismissed by the American Psychiatric Association, American Psychological Association, and American Medical Association as lacking supporting empirical or clinical evidence, and it is not included in the *Diagnostic and Statistical Manual of Mental Disorders* (DSM-5) or the International Classification of Diseases (ICD-11). In 2018, The National Council of Juvenile and Family Court Judges rejected the use of parental alienation.

BASICS OF COERCIVE CONTROL CRIMINALIZED LEGISLATION

Codifying coercive control as a form of domestic abuse is imperative—understanding abuse beyond the violent incident model. Many believe that these policies are a moral imperative, including the criminalization of coercive control as a crime against humanity. Cassandra Wiener explains in her book, *Coercive Control and the Criminal Law* (2022), how the criminal justice system creates the second layer of victimization. The first being from the abuser, the second from a system that fails to see abuse through the coercive control lens. She makes the argument that our laws need to be coercive control informed, allowing for procedures that provide a framework built to ensure the safety of victims.

STATUS IN VARIOUS COUNTRIES REGARDING CRIMINALIZING COERCIVE CONTROL LEGISLATION

In England and Wales, Ireland, and Scotland, coercive control is criminalized. It has also recently been criminalized in New South Wales and Queensland, Australia.

From a legal perspective, in most European Member States, psychological violence is prosecuted under criminal offenses that are not specific to the domestic or intimate partner context. Denmark, Spain, France, Hungary, and Ireland have implemented specific criminal offenses for psychological violence or coercive control. And only Denmark and Ireland use the language of coercive control in legislation.

The United States is woefully behind, with Hawaii the only state that has codified coercive control as a form of domestic abuse and criminalized coercive control. The bill, passed in July 2021, determines the offense of coercive control as a petty misdemeanor.

BASICS OF COERCIVE CONTROL CODIFIED LEGISLATION

Coercive control is the underpinning of domestic violence and must be codified to be included as a form of domestic violence. Codifying coercive control ensures that victims who suffer nonphysical violence are also protected.

United States: The United States has six states that have codified coercive control as a form of domestic abuse. This leaves forty-four states still using the violent incident model in determining victims' protections. These state laws have been named after female victims who have been murdered by their perpetrators—during post-separation abuse, when the coercive control intensifies (Sharps-Jeffs, Kelly, and Klein, 2017). In a review of 358 homicides in the United Kingdom, it was found that controlling or obsessive behaviors were present in 92% to 94% of the cases (Monckton-Smith, Szymanska, and Haile, 2017).

Canada: *The Divorce Act*

Under the Divorce Act of March 2021, family violence is any behavior that is violent, threatening, or a pattern of coercive and controlling behavior, or behavior that causes a family member to fear for their safety or the safety of another person. The Divorce Act includes the experiences of children as having violence and abuse directed at them, seeing or hearing someone being violent toward a family member, and seeing a family member scared or injured.

United Kingdom: *Love Bombing*

The Crown Prosecution Service (CPS), an independent body responsible for prosecuting people in England and Wales, updated their guidance relating to stalking, harassment, and controlling and coercive behavior to officially include love bombing. Love bombing is now recognized as a behavior linked to abuse and is defined as when the tactic by abuser's intermittently carrying out loving acts (e.g., sending flowers) between others to confuse the victim and gain more control (Crown Prosecution Services 2023).

IN A PERFECT WORLD . . .

Worldwide, we need to codify coercive control as a form of domestic abuse and criminalize the intentional acts of perpetrators to exert this power and control over vulnerable victims. We need the passing of legislation similar to Australia's Family Law Amendment Act, repealing a legal presumption of "equal shared parental responsibility." Additionally, we need policy aligned with VAWA with Kayden's Law, placing the physical safety and psychological well-being of children front and center, where it rightfully belongs. Parental alienation syndrome needs to be recognized as the pseudoscience it is, and court professionals need to be coercive-control trauma informed to understand all the tactics coercive controller/narcissistic abusers use to harm both adult and child victims. We need a societal shift recognizing abuse beyond the violent incident model. Domestic abuse and child abuse are not siloed issues. Children are beyond witnesses or exposed to abuse inflicted by perpetrators, experiencing the abuse in much the same way the adult victim does.

GLOBAL STATUS OF WOMEN'S RIGHTS

At the time of this writing, we are witnessing a disturbing attack on women's rights and autonomy worldwide. The gendered injustice in family courts is part of a historic discrimination against women in many of our institutions. Internationally, there have been various initiatives over the past century to eradicate the gendered oppression of women. Below are prominent examples.

- 1923: The Equal Rights Amendment (ERA) was proposed to guarantee that all citizens have the same rights, regardless of their sex, thereby ending the legal distinctions between men and women in terms of divorce, property, employment, and other matters and create full equality.

  The Equal Rights Amendment (ERA) has yet to be ratified to the Constitution, although constitutional law states that Congress has the authority to do so.

- 1981: The Convention on the Elimination of All Forms of Discrimination Against Women (CEDAW) was adopted by the United Nations General Assembly on December 18, 1979, and went into effect on September 3, 1981. The CEDAW, also known as the International Bill of Rights of Women, is an international treaty that aims to eliminate discrimination against women in all fields and spheres. The CEDAW has been acknowledged by 186 of 193 member states.

  The United States has yet to ratify CEDAW, which requires presidential support and a two-thirds vote in the Senate.

- 1993: The United Nations Declaration on the Elimination of Violence against Women defined violence against women as any act of gender-based violence that results in, or is likely to result in, physical, sexual, or psychological harm or suffering to women, including threats of such acts, coercion, or arbitrary deprivation of liberty, whether occurring in public or in private life.

- 1994: The Inter-America Convention on the Prevention, Punishment and Eradication of Violence Against Women, the "Convention of Belém do Pará," was initiated in the American States to assert among other imperatives, that violence against women constitutes a violation of their human rights and fundamental freedoms, and impairs or nullifies the observance, enjoyment, and exercise of such rights and freedoms.

  The United States and Canada are two of six American States out of thirty-four American states that have not ratified the Inter-American Convention.

- 1995: Amnesty International launched the "Human Rights are Women's Rights Campaign" in an effort to draw attention to the oppression of women worldwide.

- 2011: The Istanbul Convention, a European treaty, was adopted to end violence against women including domestic abuse. It recognizes the abuse of women as a violation of human rights and a form of discrimination requiring parties to develop interventions, including laws and policies, supporting initiatives to end all violence against women.

ACTION STEPS FOR ADVOCATES
Legislative Engagement

1) Find your legislators/parliament members who are active on victims' rights, including domestic abuse and child abuse. Individuals who have sponsored coercive control and victims' rights legislation in your country, state/province/region are ideal. And then meet with them. Write to them. Call them.

2) Research and find the advocacy groups in your area who are seeking policy reform— prioritizing the physical safety and psychological well-being of children. Collaborate with them.

3) Find your country or state's Protective Mothers' organizations. These groups can be found online and can help to galvanize efforts. They are usually women who have experienced the kind of situations relayed in this book. Join them.

4) Organize "Accountability Advocates." Accountability advocates could make a world of differ-

ence, ensuring that these laws are being followed as intended.

PHILOSOPHICAL ENGAGEMENT

1) Believe victims.
2) Understand that, due to the social political constructs of our society, women and children are the most susceptible to and defenseless against a perpetrator's exertion of power and control over them.
3) Be aware that the term *parental alienation* has been co-opted by coercive controllers/narcissistic abusers as a way to remove custody from a protective parent.
4) Engage boys and men in the conversations and create allies in this work across all spheres. This issue impacts women and children at a greater rate; however, the intergenerational trauma can be prevented by supporting both girls and boys, women and men, LGBTQ, and those who do not identify along the binary in understanding the "green flags" in a relationship—the signs that a relationship is healthy and how we should all treat one another humanely, regardless of gender identity, race, ethnicity, socioeconomic class, etc.
5) Do not judge a victim for staying. Sometimes staying feels safer. The threats by coercive controllers/narcissistic abusers are not idle. Victims know they are trapped in a variety of ways, phys-

ically, psychologically, financially, and of course, their greatest fear—having to share custody with the abuser, or lose custody to the abuser.

Finally, as mentioned earlier in this book, we hope you follow us—and so many other activists in this field—on social media. Every time you share a post, you are educating other potential allies.

10 by 10: Share what you have learned—better yet, share *FRAMED* with your network. We wrote this book not just to validate the experiences of survivors—but to shock and educate our society at large. We need supporters who may not have experienced family court themselves but feel strongly that protective parents and children need to be safe. And then ask your network to share our book or the stories with ten more people. Coercive control occurs behind closed doors and is embedded in our systems. It is an epidemic. It can only be stopped by elevating the conversation and sharing the reality of the dark underbelly of the family court underworld.

Please write a book review: When you write a review on Amazon, a bookseller's website (such as Barnes & Noble), or Goodreads, it signals to the world that this is an important topic. Then the algorithms on these sites give these mothers' stories and the book more exposure. We thank you in advance for taking a few minutes to do this.

WARNING SIGNS AND HOW YOU CAN HELP

Guidelines to Support Someone You Know Experiencing Coercive Control/Narcissistic Abuse

Listen: If possible, find a time and place that is safe and confidential to talk to your friend/family member. Start the conversation by expressing concern (i.e., "I am worried about your safety"). Allow your friend/family to speak, and let them know you believe what they are telling you.

Offer support: Let them know they are not alone and that no one deserves to be hurt. Abuse is not the victim's fault. Assure them what they are feeling is okay. Then, ask how you can best support them.

Educate yourself: Create a greater understanding of the psychological tactics of coercive control that abusers use to erode away a victim's ability to have perspective on what is actually occurring—abuse. Read up on trauma bonding so that you can better understand a victim's experiences.

Provide resources: Encourage them to reach out to community resources. Connect them with crisis hotlines, support groups, domestic violence shelters, mental health services, or anything else they may need. Safety planning may be necessary.

Respect their choices: Do not pressure them into leaving (escaping). It is never as simple as just leaving. There are many reasons people stay in an abusive relationship. Offer them support and resources, but ultimately know it is their decision.

Do not be judgmental: Do not make them feel badly for staying in an abusive relationship. Let them know you will be there for them no matter what choice they make.

Follow up with them: Do understand that it takes a great deal of courage to disclose abuse and to share experiences, particularly when the institutions betray us. Victims will feel a great deal of shame and will wonder if they are crazy or something is wrong with them. Isolation only exacerbates these feelings.

WARNING SIGNS OF AN ABUSIVE RELATIONSHIP

Coercive control can be physical but oftentimes it begins more overtly with psychological tactics, such as gaslighting, manipulation, intimidation, and isolation. These tactics, intermittent with feelings of love, create confusion and self-doubt on the part of the victim. Additionally, financial abuse and sexual abuse may occur within the relationship and continue outside of the relationship. When separation/divorce occur, legal abuse often ensues, and this is when a long-standing pattern of weaponizing the children often becomes overt. *The Women's Aid Federation of England details the signs that someone may be in an abusive relationship.*

- Isolating you from friends and family
- Depriving you of basic needs, such as food
- Monitoring your time
- Monitoring you via online communication tools or spyware
- Taking control over aspects of your everyday life, such as where you can go, who you can see, what you can wear, and when you can sleep
- Depriving you access to support services, such as medical services
- Repeatedly putting you down, such as saying you're worthless
- Humiliating, degrading, or dehumanizing you
- Controlling your finances
- Making threats or intimidating you (https://www.womensaid.org.uk/)

THE TRAUMA BOND

Many victims-survivors find it challenging to leave due to (reasonable) fear and also due to trauma bonding. According to Dutton and Painter (1981) who coined the term trauma bonding, both the imbalance of power and the intermittent abuse are needed to develop the trauma bond. This traumatic bonding causes individuals to distrust their own judgment (1993). Patrick Carnes (2016) details the seven stages of the trauma bonding cycle. These include: love bombing, trust and dependency, criticism, gaslighting, emotional addiction, loss of self, and resignation, and submission. According to Dr. Ramani, there are common patterns of trauma-bonded relationships. Perhaps someone you know is showing these common patterns.

THE 10 COMMON PATTERNS OF TRAUMA-BONDED RELATIONSHIPS

1) Justifying abusive and invalidating behavior
2) Believing the future faking
3) Experiencing chronic conflict: breaking up and making up; having the same fights
4) Characterizing the relationship as magical, metaphysical, or mystical
5) Fearing what will happen if the relationship ends
6) Becoming a one-stop supply for the narcissistic person
7) Hiding your feelings and needs
8) Rationalizing the relationship to other people or hiding the toxic patterns
9) Feeling pity and guilt for having bad thoughts about the relationship
10) Fearing conflict (Durvasula, 2024, p. 78)

TACTICS COERCIVE CONTROLLERS/

NARCISSISTIC ABUSERS USE POST SEPARATION

The Duluth Post Separation Abuse Wheel was created in 1984 through listening to the stories of women who had experienced abuse. *Duluth research (1984) concluded that systems and institutions are the foundational layer of these abuses, as depicted in the graphic found on the Domestic Abuse Interventions Program website: www.theduluthmodel.org*

The aspects of the Post Separation Abuse Wheel are listed below.

Using Harassment and Intimidation
- Destroying things belonging to her and the children
- Using children to justify breaking no-contact orders
- Threatening and stalking her and the children
- Using third parties to harass, threaten, and coerce her
- Abusing animals

Undermining Her Ability to Parent
- Disrupting children's sleep and feeding patterns
- Withholding information about children's social, emotional, and physical needs
- Contradicting her rules for children
- Demanding visitation schedule at children's expense

Discrediting Her as A Mother

- Using her social status against her—sexual identity, immigration, race, religion, education, income
- Inundating systems with false accusations of bad parenting, cheating, using drugs, and being mentally ill
- Exploiting the notion that "children need their father" to gain sympathy
- Isolating her from support by turning family and friends against her

Withholding Financial Support
- Withholding financial support, insurance, medical care, and basic expense payments
- Using court action to take her money and resources
- Interfering with her ability to work
- Blocking access to money after separation

Endangering Children
- Neglecting the children when they're with him
- Putting children in age-inappropriate emotional and physical situations
- Using violence in front of children

Disregarding Children
- Ignoring children's school schedules and homework
- Ridiculing children's needs, wants, fears, and identities
- Forcing family members, new girlfriends or wives, and other women to do his parenting work

- Treating children as younger or older than they are
- Enforcing strict gender roles

Disrupting Her Relationship with Children
- Coercing children to ally with him
- Degrading her to the children
- Using children as spies
- Isolating children from her
- Isolating her from children

Using Physical/Sexual Violence Against Mothers/Children
- Forcing sex as a condition for keeping children safe or allowing her to see them
- Threatening to kill or kidnap the children
- Abusing children physically, sexually, emotionally
- Threatening suicide
- Exposing children to pornography

ACKNOWLEDGMENTS

We acknowledge the bravest mothers everywhere suffering injustice through our family court system while simultaneously attempting to protect their children. We also want to recognize advocates everywhere—those committed to and working on the front lines supporting victims attempting to survive the dark underbelly of family court. Together we have hope that the system can be exposed. Together we believe the system can be reimagined. Together we dream that women and children will be protected from harm by coercive controllers/narcissistic abusers—but we need enough people to become enraged about stories like these in this book and demand change.

To Mom and Dad—Thank you for always believing in me. I am so grateful for your loving example in my life. And to Martin and Liv—Thank you for finding your trust in me and for being my greatest teachers. *Love you—forever and a day, Mom (Christine)*

To Max—Thank you for always being my biggest cheerleader—and for keeping me laughing along the way. *Much love, Mom (Amy)*

REFERENCES

American Psychiatric Association. 2013. Desk Reference to the Diagnostic Criteria from DSM-5 (R). Arlington, TX: American Psychiatric Association Publishing.

Amnesty International. *Report on Torture.* "Biderman's Chart of Coercion." London, England: Duckworth Publications, 1973.

Amnesty International. *Stop Violence Against Women: It's in our hands.* [Report]. London, England: Amnesty International Publications, 1995.

Angelou, Maya. *I Know Why the Caged Bird Sings.* New York, NY: Random House, 1969.

Bala, N.M.C, J.J. Paetsch, N. Trocmé, J. Schuman, S.L. Tanchak, and J.P. Hornick. "Allegations of Child Abuse in the Context of Parental Separation: A Discussion Paper." Ottawa, ON: Department of Justice Canada, 2001.

Biderman, Albert D. "Communist Attempts to Elicit False Confessions from Air Force Prisoners of War." *Bulletin of the New York Academy of Medicine* **33, no.** 9 (1957): 616–25.

Brassard, M.R., and K.L. Donovan. "Defining Psychological Maltreatment." In *Child Abuse and Neglect: Definitions, Classifications, and a Framework for Research*, edited by M.

M. Feerick, J.F. Knutson, P.K. Trickett, and S.M. Flanzer. Baltimore, MD: Paul H. Brookes Publishing Co., Inc., 2006: 3–27.

Callaghan, J.E.M., J.H. Alexander, J. Sixsmith, and L.C. Fellin. "Beyond 'Witnessing': Children's Experiences of Coercive Control in Domestic Violence and Abuse. *Journal of Interpersonal Violence* 7, no 3 (2018), 333–342.

Carrasco, Joni Dee. "False Accusations of Munchausen Syndrome by Proxy: A Mother's Experience of Persecution." PhD diss., Pacifica Graduate Institute, 2023. Publication no. 30319166. https://www.proquest.com/openview/ead-c070e5e883a29a28d3feb08c8f589/1?pq-origsite=gscholar&cbl=18750&diss=y

Carnes, Patrick. *The Betrayal Bond: Breaking Free of Exploitive Relationships*. Deerfield Beach, FL: Health Communications, Inc., 2019.

Clements, K.A.V., M. Sprecher, S. Modica et al. "The Use of Children as a Tactic of Intimate Partner Violence and its Relationship to Survivors' Mental Health." *Journal of Family Violence* 37 (2022): 1049–55. https://doi.org/10.1007/s10896-021-00330-0.

Crown Prosecution Services. "Prosecutor's Focus on 'Love-bombing' and Other Manipulative Behaviours When Charging Controlling Offences." April 24, 2023. https://www.cps.gov.uk/cps/news/prosecutors-focus-love-bombing-and-other-manipulative-behaviours-when-charging-controlling.

Dalgarno, Elizabeth, Emma Katz, Sonja Ayeb-Karlsson, Adrienne Barnett, Paola Motosi, and Arpana Verma. "'Swim, Swim and Die at the Beach': Family Court and Perpetrator Induced Trauma (CPIT) Experiences of Mothers in Brazil."

Journal of Social Welfare and Family Law 46, no. 1 (2023): 11–38. https://doi.org/10.1080/09649069.2023.2285136.

Department of International Law. "Multilateral Treaties. Inter-American Convention on the Prevention, Punishment and Eradication of Violence Against Women 'Convention of Belem do Para.'" 1994. https://www.oas.org/juridico/english/treaties/a-61.html.

Domestic Violence Abuse Intervention Project. "Post Separation Abuse Wheel." 2013. https://www.theduluth-model.org/wp-content/uploads/2017/03/Using-Children-Wheel.pdf.

Durvasula, Ramani. *It's Not You: Identifying and Healing from Narcissistic People.* New York, NY: The Open Field/Penguin Life Book, 2024.

Dutton, Don, and S. L. Painter. "Victimology: An international journal." *Victimology* 6, no. 1-4 (1981): 139-155.

Dutton, Donald G., and Susan Painter. "Emotional attachments in abusive relationships: A test of traumatic bonding theory." *Violence and victims* 8, no. 2 (1993): 105. https://doi.org/10.1891/0886-6708.8.2.105.

Feld, L., V. Glock-Molloy, and R. Stanton. "When Litigants Cry Wolf: False Reports of Child Maltreatment in Custody Litigation and How to Address Them." *NYU Journal of Legislation & Public Policy* 24, no. 1 (2021).

Fontes, Lisa. *Invisible Chains. Overcoming Coercive Control in Your Intimate Relationship.* New York, NY: Guilford Press, 2015.

Freyd, Jennifer, and Pamela Birrell. *Blind to Betrayal: Why We Fool Ourselves We Aren't Being Fooled.* Wauwatosa, WI: Trade Paper Press, 2013.

Freyd, Jennifer J. *Betrayal Trauma: The Logic of Forgetting Childhood Abuse.* Cambridge, MA: Harvard University Press, 1996.

Freyd, Jennifer J. "Violations of Power, Adaptive Blindness, and Betrayal Trauma Theory." *Feminism & Psychology* 7, no 1 (1997): 22–32.

Gardner, Richard A. "Recent Trends in Divorce and Custody Litigation." *Academy Forum* 29, no. 2 (1985): 3–7.

Gardner, Richard A. *The Parental Alienation Syndrome and the Differentiation Between Fabricated and Genuine Child Sex Abuse.* Cresskill, NJ: Creative Therapeutics, 1987.

Gardner, Richard A. *True and False Accusations of Child Sex Abuse.* Cresskill, NJ: Creative Therapeutics, 1992.

Gruev-Vintila, A. Le contrôle coercitif au cœur de la violence conjugale. *Des avancées scientifiques aux avancées juridiques.* Paris: Dunod, 2023.

Harvard Law Review. "Judicial Immunity at the (Second) Founding: A New Perspective on § 1983." *Harvard Law Review* 136, no. 5 (March 2023):1456–76.

Herman, Judith, L. *Truth and Repair: How Trauma Survivors Envision Justice.* New York, NY: Basic Books, 2023.

hooks, bell. *Feminist Theory: From Margin to Center,* 3rd ed. London, England: Routledge Publishing, 2015.

Jaffe, P., Nicholas Bala, Archana Medhekar, Katreena, L. Scott, and Casey Oliver. "Making Appropriate Parenting Arrangements in Family Violence Cases: Applying the Literature to Identify Promising Practices, 2023." Department of Justice Canada, 2023.

Joh-Carnella, N., E. Livingston, M. Kagan-Cassidy, A. Vandermorris, J.N. Smith, D.M. Lindberg, and B. Fallon. "Understanding the Roles of the Healthcare and Child Welfare Systems in Promoting the Safety and Well-being of Children. *Frontiers in Psychiatry* 14 (2023): 1195440.

Katz, C.C., C. Pisciotta, R. Hajjar, E.V. Wall, and V. Lens. "Navigating a Flawed System: An Investigation of the Strategies Employed by Legal Teams in Family Court. *Family Court Review* 61, no. 2 (2023): 287–303. https://doi.org/10.1111/fcre.12707.

Katz, E. Beyond the Physical Incident Model: How Children Living with Domestic Violence are Harmed By and Resist Regimes of Coercive Control. *Child Abuse Rev.*, 25: (2016): 46–59. https://doi.org/10.1002/car.2422.

Katz, Emma. "From 'Parental Alienation' to (Abusers') Child and Mother Sabotage." Decoding Coercive Control with Dr. Emma Katz. October 23, 2023. https://dremmakatz.substack.com/p/from-parental-alienation-to-abusers.

Katz, Emma. *Coercive Control in Children's and Mothers' Lives.* New York, NY: Oxford University Press, 2022.

Kerns, Robert. "Crying Wolf: The Use of False Accusations of Abuse to Influence Child Custodianship and a Proposal to Protect the Innocent." *South Texas Law Review* 56, no. 4 (2015). https://doi.org/10.2139/ssrn.2715774.

Lapierre, S., I. Côté, A. Lambert, D. Buetti, C. Lavergne, D. Damant, and V. Couturier. "Difficult but Close Relationships: Children's Perspectives on Relationships with Their Mothers in the Context of Domestic Violence." *Violence Against Women* 24, no. 9 (2018): 1023–38. https://doi.org/10.1177/1077801217731541.

Lee, Bandy. "How Many Children Will Jane Gallina-Mecca Sacrifice before She Is Held Accountable?" Medium. May 7, 2024. https://bandyxlee.medium.com/how-many-children-will-jane-gallina-mecca-sacrifice-before-she-is-held-accountable-64b072653634.

Manne, Kate. *Down Girl: The Logic of Misogyny.* New York, NY: Oxford University Press, 2018.

McManus, S., S. Walby, E.C. Barbosa, L. Appleby, T. Brugha, P.E. Bebbington, E.A. Cook, and D. Knipe. "Intimate Partner Violence, Suicidality, and Self-harm: A Probability Sample Survey of the General Population in England." *Lancet Psychiatry* 9, no. 7 (July 2022): 574–83. https://doi.org/10.1016/S2215-0366(22)00151-1.

Meier, Joan S., Sean Dickson, Chris O'Sullivan, Leora Rosen, and Jeffrey Hayes. "Child Custody Outcomes in Cases Involving Parental Alienation and Abuse Allegations" (2019). GWU Law School Public Law Research Paper No. 2019-56, GWU Legal Studies Research Paper No. 2019–56. http://dx.doi.org/10.2139/ssrn.3448062.

Mennicke, Annelise, M., and Katie Ropes. "Estimating the Rate of Domestic Violence Perpetrated by Law Enforcement Officers: A Review of Methods and Estimates." *Aggression and Violent Behavior* 31 (2016): 157–64. https://doi.org/10.1016/j.avb.2016.09.003.

Miller, Susan, and Nicole Smolter. "'Paper Abuse': When All Else Fails, Batterers Use Procedural Stalking." *Violence Against Women* 17, no. 5 (2011): 637–50. https://doi.org/10.1177/1077801211407290.

Monckton-Smith, J., K. Szymanska, and S. Haile. "Exploring the Relationship between Stalking and Homicide." Project report. University of Gloucestershire in association with Suzy Lamplugh Trust, Cheltenham, 2017.

Nicholson, S.B., and D.J. Lutz. "The Importance of Cognitive Dissonance in Understanding and Treating Victims of Intimate Partner Violence. *Journal of Aggression, Maltreatment & Trauma* 26, no. 5 (2017): 475–92.

Nugent, Ciara. "'Abuse Is a Pattern.' Why These Nations Took the Lead in Criminalizing Controlling Behavior." *Time*. June 21, 2019. https://time.com/5610016/coercive-control-domestic-violence.

Relating to Domestic Violence, Hawaii Revised Statutes. § 709–906 (6) (2021). https://legiscan.com/HI/text/HB2067/id/2169368.

Rennison, Callie Marie. "Intimate Partner Violence and Age of Victim." Bureau of Justice Statistics: Intimate Partner Violence. October 2001. https://bjs.ojp.gov/content/pub/pdf/ipva99.pdf.

Rice, J., C.M. West, K. Cottman, and G. Gardner. "The Intersectionality of Intimate Partner Violence in the Black Community." In *Handbook of Interpersonal Violence and Abuse Across the Lifespan*, edited by R. Geffner, J.W. White, L.K. Hamberger, A. Rosenbaum, V. Vaughan-Eden, and V.I. Vieth. Switzerland: Springer, Cham, 2022. https://doi.org/10.1007/978-3-319-89999-2_240.

Rosenfeld, Esther, and Michelle Oberman with Jordan Bernard and Erika Lee. "Confronting the Challenge of the High-Conflict Personality in Family Court." *Family Law Quarterly* 53, no. 2 (2019): 79–118.

Saunders, D. G., K.C. Faller, and R.M. Tolman. "Beliefs and Recommendations Regarding Child Custody and Visitation in Cases Involving Domestic Violence: A Comparison of Professionals in Different Roles." *Violence Against Women* 22, no. 6 (2016): 722–44. https://doi.org/10.1177/1077801215608845.

Sgambelluri, R. "Police Culture, Police Training, and Police Administration: Their Impact on Violence in Police Families," In *Domestic Violence by Police Officers*, edited by D.C. Sheehan, 309–22. US Government, Washington, DC, 2000.

Sharp-Jeffs, Nicola, Liz Kelly, and Renate Klein. "Long Journeys toward Freedom: The Relationship between Coercive Control and Space for Action—Measurement and Emerging Evidence. *Violence Against Women* 24, no. 2 (February 2, 2017): 163–85. https://doi.org/10.1177/1077801216686199.

Simonic, Barbara and Elżbieta Osweska. "Traumatic Bonding in Intimate Partner Violence: A Relational Family Therapy Approach. *The Journal of Family Forum* (2019). https://doi.org/ 10.25167/FF/1092.

Sousa Filho, D., E.Y. Kanomata, R.J. Feldman, and A. Maluf Neto. "Munchausen Syndrome and Munchausen Syndrome by Proxy: A Narrative Review." *Einstein (Sao Paulo, Brazil)* 15, no. 4 (2017): 516–21. https://doi.org/10.1590/S1679-45082017MD3746.

Stark, Evan, and Marianne Hester. "Coercive Control: Update and Review." *Violence Against Women,* 25, no 1. (2019), 81–104. https://doi.org/10.1177/1077801218816191.

Stark, Evan. *Children of Coercive Control.* New York, NY: Oxford University Press, 2023.

Stark, Evan. *Coercive Control: How Men Entrap Women in Personal Life.* New York, NY: Oxford University Press, 2007.

Stark, Evan. "Re-presenting Battered Women: Coercive Control and the Defense on Liberty [Paper presentation]." Violence Against Women: Complex Realities and New Issues in a Changing World. Les Presses de l'Université du Québec,

2012. https://www.stopvaw.org/uploads/evan_stark_article_ final_100812.pdf.

Stephens, T.N., C.C. Katz, C. Pisciotta, and V. Lens. "The View from the Other Side: How Parents and Their Representatives View Family Court. *Family Court Review* 59, no. 3 (2021): 491–507. https://doi.org/10.1111/fcre.12590.

Thomas, R.M., and J.T. Richardson. "Parental Alienation Syndrome: 30 Years On and Still Junk Science." *Judges Journal* 54 no. 3 (2015): 22–4.

Wiener, Cassandra. *Coercive Control and the Criminal Law.* New York, NY: Routledge Publishing, 2022.

Women's Aid Federation of England. "What Is Coercive Control?" Accessed Feb 8, 2024. www.https://www.womensaid.org.uk/information-support/what-is-domestic-abuse/coercive-control/.

World Health Organization. "Violence Against Women [Fact Sheet]." March 25, 2024. https://www.who.int/news-room/fact-sheets/detail/violence-against-women.

Zaccour, Suzanne. "Crazy Women and Hysterical Mothers: The Gendered Use of Mental-Health Labels in Custody Disputes." *Journal of Family Law* 31, 1 (2018): 57–103.

Zaccour, Suzanne. "Parental Alienation in Quebec Custody Litigation." *Les Cahiers de droit* 59, no. 4 (2018): 1073–11. https://doi.org/10.7202/1055264ar.

ABOUT THE AUTHORS

CHRISTINE MARIE COCCHIOLA, DSW, LCSW is an expert on the experiences of adult and child victims of coercive control. She is a college professor teaching social work for over twenty years, and has been a social justice advocate since the age of nineteen, volunteering for a local domestic violence/sexual assault agency. She received her doctorate in clinical social work from New York University, working under the tutelage of Dr. Evan Stark researching the experiences of adult and child victims of coercive control. As a survivor, protective parent, and researcher, she has utilized her clinical expertise as a trauma trained therapist creating programs to educate protective parents, attorneys, court professionals, coaches, and advocates. Her Protective Parenting Program guides protective parents on fortifying their attachment with children harmed by an abusive parent. She educates on these topics on her YouTube channel and as a host of the Perfect Prey Podcast. Dr. C is an invited guest, speaking internationally on the topic of coercive control and also testifies in support of legislation for the protections of adult and child victims of coercive control. She makes her home in Connecticut's Litchfield Hills. Learn more about Dr. C here: www.coercivecontrolconsulting.com.

AMY POLACKO is a divorce and post-separation abuse coach, who supports women before, during, and after divorce through her business Freedom Warrior. She is a Master Certified Life Coach and a Certified Divorce Specialist through the National Association of Divorce Professionals. She is a domestic abuse survivor and protective parent. Amy is also an award-winning journalist who worked on *Newsday's* Pulitzer Prize winning team covering the TWA Flight 800 crash. She holds a master's degree from Columbia University's Graduate School of Journalism and also earned an Edward R. Murrow Award, Investigative Reporter and Editors Award and multiple Associated Press Association Awards for her work. As a freelance journalist, she writes about divorce, domestic abuse, coercive control, and family court. Her work has appeared in *HuffPost, Ms., Newsweek, The Independent, Observer,* and *The Washington Post.* She created a digital course for women considering or going through divorce called "Divorce Decoded: Your Path to Freedom" which helps them navigate family court and avoid potential mistakes. Amy lives in Fairfield County, Connecticut. Learn more about Amy here: www.freedomwarrior. info.